What Readers Are Saying About *Pragmatic Guide to Sass*

Pragmatic Guide to Sass is a snappy little book that effectively hits you with the right dose of Sass magic to either pick up Sass as a newcomer or give you a refresher if you're already using it. The guide is written in a style that's both a tutorial and a reference at the same time, and it'll be a handy go-to book for anyone working with Sass, whether on a daily basis or only on rare occasions. It gets two thumbs-up from me.

➤ **Peter Cooper, editor of *Ruby Inside* and *HTML5 Weekly***

Sass is the best way to write maintainable CSS. This Pragmatic guide will get you up to speed on Sass's most powerful features, including nesting, variables, and mixins—an invaluable reference.

➤ **Sam Stephenson, creator of Sprockets and the Rails asset pipeline**

Michael and Hampton, in *Pragmatic Guide to Sass,* have put together the most comprehensive and thought-out guide to Sass to date. No matter what server-side technology you use, Sass can be used in anyone's development stack to help organize your CSS. *Pragmatic Guide to Sass* shows you the best practices in DRYing up your CSS with the power of Sass. It teaches you how to become a CSS heavyweight without the bloated CSS. This book should be on every web developer's shelf (and e-reader).

➤ **Andrew Chalkley, technical writer, Screencasts.org**

Chock-full of unexpected goodies such as extras on Compass and Haml, *Pragmatic Guide to Sass* is hands-down the best Sass resource printed to date—a must-read for web developers and smart designers.

➤ **Dan Kissell, Codenicely.com**

Pragmatic Guide to Sass

Hampton Catlin
Michael Lintorn Catlin

The Pragmatic Bookshelf

Dallas, Texas • Raleigh, North Carolina

Many of the designations used by manufacturers and sellers to distinguish their products are claimed as trademarks. Where those designations appear in this book, and The Pragmatic Programmers, LLC was aware of a trademark claim, the designations have been printed in initial capital letters or in all capitals. The Pragmatic Starter Kit, The Pragmatic Programmer, Pragmatic Programming, Pragmatic Bookshelf, PragProg and the linking *g* device are trademarks of The Pragmatic Programmers, LLC.

Every precaution was taken in the preparation of this book. However, the publisher assumes no responsibility for errors or omissions, or for damages that may result from the use of information (including program listings) contained herein.

Our Pragmatic courses, workshops, and other products can help you and your team create better software and have more fun. For more information, as well as the latest Pragmatic titles, please visit us at *http:/pragprog.com*.

The team that produced this book includes:

Kay Keppler (editor)
Potomac Indexing, LLC (indexer)
Molly McBeath (copyeditor)
David J Kelly (typesetter)
Janet Furlow (producer)
Juliet Benda (rights)
Ellie Callahan (support)

Printed in the United States of America.
ISBN-13: 978-1-934356-84-5
Printed on acid-free paper.
Book version: P1.0—December 2011

Contents

Part III — Compass

Part IV — Blueprint CSS

Acknowledgments

We'd both like to thank the entire team at Pragmatic, who are a great bunch of people to work with. They made the process of writing really enjoyable. In particular, our editor, Kay Keppler, and managing editor, Susannah Pfalzer, were personable and always on hand to answer our most inane questions.

We'd also like to thank our tech reviewers: Peter Cooper, Eric Redmond, Shawn Allison, Jeff Patzer, Trevor Burnham, Bruce Williams, Aaron Godin, and Ian Dees. Your insights were extremely useful.

Hampton: Most importantly, I'd like to thank Nathan Weizenbaum, whose endless hours of coding and bug fixes and extensions make Sass what it is today. And I can't forget Chris Eppstein, whose creation of Compass truly changed the Sass landscape forever.

Michael: Thanks to my parents, Alan and Jayne, for not giving me too much grief over stopping my PhD. Final thanks go to the GMO for keeping us sane.

Welcome!

Welcome to the *Pragmatic Guide to Sass*. Sass (Syntactically Awesome Style Sheets) enables you to do amazing things with your style sheets, helping you describe how HTML is laid out on a web page. Sass is an alternative way of writing CSS.

"What's wrong with regular ol' CSS?" we hear you cry. The fact is that CSS, with all its power and elegance, is missing some crucial, simple elements that other types of development take for granted. CSS can also be a bit complicated to read: Sass fixes that.

Most programmers are familiar with the concept of *DRY*— Don't Repeat Yourself. It saves time and effort when writing code. A core philosophy of Sass is to reduce repetition in style sheets, and we'll be coming back to DRY a few times throughout the guide.

Sass isn't really a replacement for CSS—it's a way to help us write better CSS files, which is essential for large projects. Sass helps us write clear, semantic style sheets. Sass updates CSS development for the future.

Hampton originally designed Sass while he was working at Unspace in Toronto, and Nathan Weizenbaum and Chris Eppstein now maintain it. A lot of Sass functionality depends on Ruby. (But don't worry, we'll learn how to install Ruby in Part I, *Basics*, on page 3.)

In this book, we'll be using the word Sass as an overarching concept that describes the engine we use to convert our files into CSS. We can use two syntaxes to write Sass—SCSS and Original Sass. These will be described a bit later in this preface.

Who Is This Book For?

This book is for people who know the pain of working on the CSS of a mature website—who have faced a CSS file that four people wrote and that mutated into a huge, sprawling, incoherent mess. We've looked the beast in the eye and barely survived.

You're probably already familiar with CSS, HTML, and the ideals of semantic web development. We can all agree that markup should be about logic instead of about presentation (as much as possible). And we'll assume that you're familiar with margins, padding, the box model, @media queries, and the myriad of other CSS-related technologies.

If you are looking for a CSS-ninja power-up, you've come to the right place.

Nomenclature and Syntax

Some of the terms associated with CSS can be quite confusing, so we've added a short introduction to how we name things in the book. Also, there are two different syntaxes for writing Sass that need to be distinguished.

A Brief CSS Recap

We thought it would be useful to go through a couple of technical terms we'll be using for different aspects of CSS markup. If you're already familiar with selectors, declaration blocks, and the like, you can probably skip this part.

Let's use a small bit of CSS as an example:

```
p {
  color: #336699;
  font-size: 2em;
}
```

Here we have p, which we call the *selector*. What follows (the bit inside the curly braces) is the *declaration block*. The two lines—one defining the color and one defining the font size—are known as *declarations*. Each declaration has a *property* and a *value*. The property in this case is the color or the font size. The value is the color itself—for example, *#336699*, blue—or the size of the font—for example, *20px*.

The use of *classes* and *IDs* allows us to define sets of declarations that will only be applied to specific sections of our HTML. Sass allows you to create much richer selectors, as we'll see in Part I, *Basics*, on page 3.

SCSS: A More CSS-like Way to Write Sass

SCSS, which stands for *Sassy CSS*, is one of the syntaxes we use to write Sass. The grand aim of SCSS is to keep the look of CSS while introducing the units of Sass. If you're familiar with CSS, it's pretty easy to read. We still use selectors, classes, and IDs. We open a curly brace to start the declaration block, and we separate out declarations with semicolons. What's extra is the added functionality.

When we use the word *Sass*, we'll mostly be referring to the SCSS syntax.

Original Sass: A Stripped-down Way to Write Sass

Before SCSS, there was Original Sass, which strips out some of the unnecessary elements of CSS and SCSS. Original Sass can be compiled just the same as SCSS, via the Sass engine.

A great example of unnecessary elements are curly braces. Look at this:

```
.fab_text {
  color: #336699;
  font-size: 2em; }
```

We know by the use of . or # that something is a selector. Using *whitespace* (two spaces or a soft tab that indents the properties) helps us. In the example above, the indentation lets us know that color and font-size refer only to the fab_text class. The curly braces aren't needed. Why not just strip them out?

```
.fab_text
  color: #336699;
  font-size: 2em;
```

Look at that! Doesn't the code already look a lot cleaner, a lot simpler?

While we're at it, we might as well take away the semicolons at the end of the values. They don't add much, do they?

```
.fab_text
  color: #336699
  font-size: 2em
```

And this is how Original Sass is written. As you can see, it's more different from CSS than from SCSS, as it involves removing bits we're used to. So in the examples we use in the book, we'll mostly be using SCSS to describe things. Once you're used to it, though, Original Sass should be more readable at a quick glance.

Aside from the curly braces and semicolons, most of the features we'll look at are written the same in both SCSS and Original Sass. When they're not, we'll point out how they differ. It's really up to you whether you use SCSS or Original Sass syntax.

Overview

In Part I, *Basics*, on page 3, we'll take you through the very first things you'll need to know about Sass and SCSS, like how to install (Task 1, *Installing Sass*, on page 4). We'll also take you through variables, where Sass gets really exciting (Task 9, *Defining Variables*, on page 20).

We'll take things to the next level in Part II, *Advanced*, on page 35. One of the main things we'll look at is mixins (Task 16, *Keeping Code Clean with Mixins*, on page 38). We'll also take a look at some more programmer-style functions of Sass, such as @each and @if (in Task 22, *Stop Repeating Yourself with @each*, on page 50, and Task 23, *Determining Conditions with @if*, on page 52, respectively).

Chris Eppstein's Compass is a great way to style pages, and we'll go through it in Part III, *Compass*, on page 59. We'll cover things like adding columns to your text (Task 33, *Jazzing Up Layouts with Columns*, on page 78) and making a sticky footer (Task 29, *Sticking a Footer to a Window*, on page 70).

In Part IV, *Blueprint CSS*, on page 85, we'll look at a framework that makes things even simpler than Compass. Among other things, it provides a great predefined structure to help you customize buttons, which we describe in Task 37, *Making Beautiful Buttons*, on page 90.

How to Read This Book

The book is arranged into tasks. These are short snippets of information. On the left you'll find a description of the task at hand. On the right you'll find the code you need to write to get results.

We've tried to arrange the book to go from the most basic tasks to the most advanced. However, you can definitely dip in and out of the book if you find a specific task you need to look at. Once you've grasped the very basics (such as installing), you'll probably be set to do most of the tasks in the book.

Getting Help

There are several ways you can find help for your Sass troubles. For example, join the Sass Lang Google group.[1] Also, the Sass documentation has a wealth of information that covers most of what we look at in this guide and even goes over a few other things as well.[2]

In addition, if you ever need help with the sass command, just type sass --help and Sass will let you know about all the available ways to run it.

A Few Final Comments

We're almost ready to start, but here are some little bits that you'll probably find useful to know before we dive into the book.

- We'll be using the following phrase to show when we've converted some Sass into CSS.

  This compiles to:

  Hopefully, you'll be more familiar with the CSS output, so you can easily compare how much simpler Sass is compared to CSS.

- If you've downloaded the ebook, you'll notice that all the code samples are preceded by a little shaded box. If you click on the box, the code sample shown in the book

---

1.   http://groups.google.com/group/sass-lang
2.   http://sass-lang.com/docs/yardoc/file.SASS_REFERENCE.html

will be downloaded to your computer, allowing you to play around with our examples.

- You can get more information from the book's official web page.[3] There you'll find resources such as the book forum, code downloads, and any errata.

OK—now we've got all that out of the way, are you ready to get Sassy?

---

3.   http://pragprog.com/book/pg_sass/pragmatic-guide-to-sass

Part I

Basics

Let's get going. Here's a quick run-down of what we'll be going through in the Basics section:

- We'll start by looking at how to install Sass in Task 1, *Installing Sass*, on page 4, then we'll look at how to convert a Sass file to a CSS file in Task 2, *Compiling Sass into CSS*, on page 6.

- Check out the next task for how to work with Sass in Task 3, *Using Sass with Rails*, on page 8.

- If you're not familiar with the command line, we'll look at a great Sass interface in Task 4, *Avoiding the Command Line: Using Scout*, on page 10.

- We'll look at how to do comments in Sass in Task 5, *Commenting*, on page 12.

- Then we're going to look at the idea of scoping and how this is much simpler in Sass. Scoping is introduced in Task 6, *Selector Scoping*, on page 14; we expand upon it in Task 7, *Going Further with Advanced Scoping*, on page 16.

- Learning how to change the exact CSS produced from your style sheets is covered in Task 8, *Altering the CSS Output*, on page 18.

- Then we'll move on to variables in Task 9, *Defining Variables*, on page 20.

- We'll put the skills we learned about variables to use in Task 10, *Calculating a Layout*, on page 22, and Task 11, *Creating Themes with Advanced Colors*, on page 24.

- Next we'll look at how importing can keep your style sheets cleaner and more semantic in Task 12, *Importing*, on page 26.

- In the last tasks, we'll look at a couple of ways you can use importing in Task 13, *Building a Font Family Library*, on page 28, and Task 14, *Resetting CSS*, on page 30.

1   Installing Sass

So before you can explore the simplicity (and beauty) of Sass, you'll need to set a few things up. It's useful to have a folder where you keep all your Sass files for a project. Creating a Sass file couldn't be easier: just use the extension .scss—or .sass for an Original Sass file.

The only tool you need is a text editor. Every OS comes with *something*, but of course that's not always the best something. Generally, just use whatever you usually use to write CSS. We recommend some text editors with each set of installation instructions.

In order to install and run Sass, you need to have Ruby installed on your system. We'll go through how to do this in the three major OS categories. If you're not comfortable with the command line, you may want to check out Task 4, *Avoiding the Command Line: Using Scout*, on page 10.

Installation on Windows

Because Windows doesn't come with Ruby, you'll need to install it. There are a few installers around the Internet, but we prefer the simple one at RubyInstaller.[4]

Once Ruby has been installed, you need to access the command line. Go to Start, then Accessories, then find Command Prompt. That should open a window that will allow you to run the needed install commands. A decent text editor for Windows is Notepad++.

Installation on a Mac

Unlike Windows, Ruby is already installed on OS X, making things a bit easier. All we need to do is open the Terminal application and install Sass via the command line. The text editor that we use on our Macs is TextMate.

Installation for Linux

If you're a Linux user, you'll be aware of how to access your command line—we won't insult your Unix-fu. To install Ruby (and Ruby gems), use your package manager. We recommend Ruby version 1.9.2. As for text editors, Vim tends to be the most popular.

---

4.   http://rubyinstaller.org

➤ Use this command to install Sass.

```
gem install sass
```

➤ Create a simple Sass file.

Name a file test.scss with the following contents:

```
.red {
  color: red;
}
```

➤ Test that Sass is working.

Navigate to the folder containing the test.scss file via the command line and you should see the following if you run the command sass test.scss.

```
$> sass test.scss
.red {
  color: red; }
```

It just reformatted the CSS we wrote above. Now we're ready to show you how to rock some Sass superpowers.

2   Compiling Sass into CSS

We've introduced the idea that Sass is an advanced version of CSS. As a matter of fact, *any* valid CSS is valid Sass. Sass just adds features on top of CSS—it's a kind of meta language. Unfortunately at this point, no browsers support Sass files directly, so we have to convert from Sass into CSS first.

The basic gist is that we write some Sass and then we *compile*—or convert—Sass into CSS. How do we compile Sass into CSS? Well, you did it in the last step of Task 1, *Installing Sass*, on page 4, but we didn't use any of the extra powers of Sass, so the results were pretty similar.

Let's run through how we can convert a Sass file into a CSS file again in a lot more detail than we did in the last task.

First, we need to create a Sass file. Any old thing will do—this is just to show how we can turn our Sass into CSS. Since CSS is valid Sass, take any random CSS file you have sitting around and change its extension to .scss.

Now, let's go to our command line. Type sass, followed by the name of your file.

Look at that! Oh right, it just printed out the CSS but in a different format. And printing out your CSS files to the console isn't very useful. It would be better if we could make a separate CSS file.

Well, you can! Run the sass command again with a second argument that specifies the output file you want. For instance, you might say sass test.scss test.css and Sass will generate a CSS file named test.css.

Running that command over and over would be extremely tedious as we edit our Sass file. If you are using Rails or another framework, it can automatically update your CSS for you. But when we aren't using a framework, we have a neat command-line trick for converting Sass files into CSS files as we alter them. It's called watch.

watch will take any .scss file found in the specified Sass folder and convert it into a .css file in the specified CSS folder. Magic! It doesn't just do this once either. It constantly *watches* the file for any changes and incorporates them into the CSS file.

Another useful command to mention here is convert. You can use this to turn a .css file into a .sass or .scss file.

➤ Start with a simple bit of Sass.

```
.fab_text {
  color: #336699;
  font-size: 2em;
}
```

➤ Type this in your command line.

```
sass fabtext.scss
```

You should see the following:

```
.fab_text {
  color: #336699;
  font-size: 2em; }
```

➤ Watch a folder.

Assuming we have a Sass and a CSS folder, the command would look like this:

```
sass --watch stylesheets/sass:stylesheets/css
```

➤ Convert a CSS file to a Sass file.

```
sass convert test.css test.sass
```

Related Tasks:

- Task 8, *Altering the CSS Output,* on page 18

3   Using Sass with Rails

Sass was originally built to work with Rails, and it's painfully easy to use with the popular Ruby web framework. If you don't use Rails, then move on to the next chapter, where we'll show you an easy way to work with Sass files on your computer. The only difficult part is dealing with the slight differences between Rails versions. But read on, brave reader, and we'll get you sorted out.

If you are using a Rails version previous to 3.0, then all you need to do to get Sass working with your Rails application is to add config.gem 'sass' to your environment.rb file. If you place your Sass files inside of public/stylesheets/sass/ (yes, make sure to make the directory!), then they will automatically get compiled to CSS in the public/stylesheets/ folder.

In Rails 3.0 the process is very similar, but instead of config.gem, we use the Gemfile and add the line gem 'sass'. Bundler makes it easy, as usual!

In Rails 3.1+, Sass is included! Seriously! You don't have to do anything specific. Just installing Rails 3.1 installs Sass, but the process for working with Sass is a little different due to the introduction of the *asset pipeline* into Rails. The asset pipeline includes both Sass and CoffeeScript, a Javascript replacement language that supports many advanced features like asset compression, bundling, and more. Covering these features is outside of the scope of this quick book, but in general Rails will generate an .scss file with every controller and will place it in app/assets/stylesheets. You can find out more about Rails 3.1's asset handling at the Rails site.[5]

---

5.   Rails Edge Guide to the Asset Pipeline: http://edgeguides.rubyonrails.org/asset_pipeline.html

➤ **Install with Rails older than 3.0.**

Add this line to your config/environment.rb file.

```
config.gem 'sass'
```

Since we aren't using Bundler here, you have to make sure the Sass gem is installed on your system, which we cover in Task 1, *Installing Sass*, on page 4.

```
gem install sass
```

➤ **Install with Rails 3.0.**

Add this line to your Gemfile.

```
gem 'sass'
```

Then make sure to run bundle!

```
bundle install
```

➤ **Use on Rails 2.0 or 3.0.**

First, start up your Rails server. Then, create a public/stylesheets/sass/application.scss file and put some simple SCSS inside it.

```
.worked {
  width: 100;
}
```

If you load a page on your Rails application, then public/stylesheets/application.css should contain the exact contents as application.scss. It will auto reload this file every time you make a change to the SCSS file. So make sure not to edit the CSS file or else you will be sad when it gets replaced!

4   Avoiding the Command Line: Using Scout

So far we've been using the command line to generate our CSS from Sass. However, not everyone is comfortable using the command line. A great app to help you use Sass (and Compass, a tool we'll come across in Part III, *Compass*, on page 59) is Scout.[6]

Scout is a graphical user interface (GUI) that automatically sorts out all the Ruby installation stuff we've been describing in the previous tasks. You don't need to know about the command line at all.

Once we've downloaded Scout, we just import our project file. We specify the input folder, which is typically our Sass folder. Then we specify the output folder, which is usually the stylesheet folder. Hit the play button, and Scout watches your Sass files.

As soon as you make a change to a Sass file, Scout notices and updates the corresponding CSS file in your output folder. It's really that simple!

---

6.   http://mhs.github.com/scout-app/

➤ Import your project and set up your input and output folders.

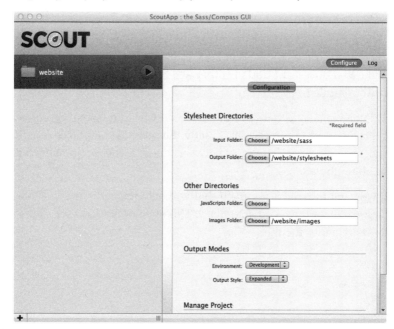

➤ Scout logs your changes.

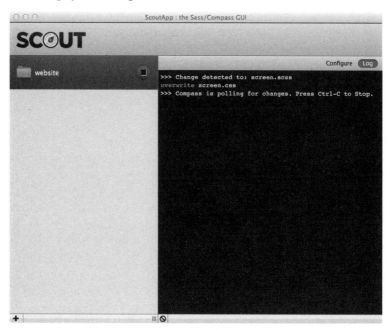

5   Commenting

Comments are snippets of text that are ignored by the browser. Sass gives us the option of two types of comments. One will only show up in the Sass document, and the other will be incorporated into the CSS that's compiled.

The comment style that's compiled into the CSS is the same one you're probably used to—in fact, it's exactly the same as the CSS comment style. Just place your comment between /* and */. These comments can be on multiple lines.

If we want to write a comment that will only appear in the Sass file, then we place the comment after //. This style only works for single-line comments, though.

➤ Use two different styles of comments.

basics/comments.scss

```scss
/* Hey look at this multiline comment
 * that we want to show up in our CSS
 * output. */

#page {
  color: black; }

// These comments are single lines
// and we do not want them to appear
// in our CSS

#sidebar {
  color: #336699; }
```

This compiles to:

```css
/* Hey look at this multiline comment
 * that we want to show up in our CSS
 * output. */
#page {
  color: black; }

#sidebar {
  color: #336699; }
```

6 Selector Scoping

Let's look at a core feature of Sass: nesting. If you've been working with CSS for a long time, you know the advantages of giving more specific selectors to your style sheets. Using .sidebar p em allows you greater specificity to the em element versus a standalone em selector. It gives you more freedom with reusing names and making your HTML more semantic and readable. We generally refer to this as *scoping*.

It's a good thing to scope, except it's not DRY. (Remember *D*on't *R*epeat *Y*ourself?). We keep having to repeat our classes or IDs—for example, repeating an apply-to-all class like .infobox—on every line. Typing this by hand is laborious and makes us want to be lazy. When writing CSS, scoping can be very tedious. It involves a lot of copying and pasting. What's more, keeping track of parent-child relationships is tough. We can do better than that! Technology should support good behaviors. Sass is here to help us with *nesting*.

We can put a style such as a border color *inside* a declaration block, and Sass will automatically do the repetitive part for you when you generate CSS. I bet your fingers are thanking you already for saving all that typing. Cool, huh?

A small note: the CSS that's compiled in the example opposite looks a bit funny, doesn't it? Especially when we compare it to the original (repetitive) CSS example we wrote out. What happens is that the Sass engine keeps the indentation when it converts to CSS. All it does is insert the missing selectors.

➤ Look at this scoped CSS.

Look how much repetition there is in this file. Holy cow!

```
basics/scoping.css
.infobox                { width: 200px; }
.infobox .message       { border: 1px solid red; }
.infobox .message .title { color: red; }
.infobox .user          { border: 2px solid black; }
.infobox .user .title   { color: black; }
```

➤ See it in Sass.

Instead of repeating it, just nest it inside the parent selector.

```
basics/example_nesting.scss
.infobox {
  width: 200px;
  .message {
    border: 1px solid red;
    .title {
      color: red; } }
  .user {
    border: 2px solid black;
    .title {
      color: black; } } }
```

This compiles to:

```
.infobox {
  width: 200px; }
  .infobox .message {
    border: 1px solid red; }
    .infobox .message .title {
      color: red; }
  .infobox .user {
    border: 2px solid black; }
    .infobox .user .title {
      color: black; }
```

Related Tasks:

- Task 7, *Going Further with Advanced Scoping*, on page 16
- Task 8, *Altering the CSS Output*, on page 18

7 Going Further with Advanced Scoping

In the last section, we introduced simple nesting. Just throw a selector inside a declaration block and BAM! It automatically scopes the style as being the child of the parent. However, sometimes we need to be more explicit. The last example we gave didn't specify that the children were *direct* children. In standard CSS, we specify this directness as parent > child. If your CSS is rusty, that means finding a tag named <child> who's exactly one level inside of a <parent> tag.

Using these kinds of CSS operators is as simple as you'd hope. Just start the child selector with the operator you want. So the child would be defined as > child inside of the parent definition.

Using nesting is a great way to organize your styles. It means that all of the related styles are grouped together. By default, every child selector is the parent selector *plus* the child selector. In situations where we want to do something more advanced, we use the & selector. Simply put, & means "the parent selector." Don't look scared. It's easy stuff once it clicks.

Oftentimes, we use a bit of Javascript to add classes to the <body> tag based on what browser the user is using. For instance, if you visit with Safari, the <body> will have the classes .safari and .webkit. So when we're styling the sidebar, we might want to add a rule that says, "If the body tag has this class, apply this rule," and it would be nice to have this code near all the related rules. So if we're inside of .sidebar .item and then we write the child selector body.webkit &, Sass will compile into body.webkit .sidebar .item.

The ampersand got replaced with .sidebar .item, which was the parent's scope. If it's still a bit foggy, read over the examples. Then it should click. It really is simple!

➤ Define direct ancestors.

basics/direct_ancestors.scss

```scss
.infobox > {
  .message {
    border: 1px solid red;
    > .title {
      color: red; } }
  .user {
    border: 1px solid black;
    > .title {
      color: black; } } }
```

This compiles to:

```scss
.infobox > .message {
  border: 1px solid red; }
  .infobox > .message > .title {
    color: red; }
.infobox > .user {
  border: 1px solid black; }
  .infobox > .user > .title {
    color: black; }
```

➤ Use the magical &.

basics/ampersand_example.scss

```scss
.infobox {
  color: blue;
  .user & {
    color: gray; } }
.message {
  color: gray;
  &.new {
    color: red; } }
.infobox {
  .user & .message {
    content: "Selector is '.user .infobox .message'"; } }
```

This compiles to:

```scss
.infobox {
  color: blue; }
  .user .infobox {
    color: gray; }
.message {
  color: gray; }
  .message.new {
    color: red; }
.user .infobox .message {
  content: "Selector is '.user .infobox .message'"; }
```

8 Altering the CSS Output

When you compile your Sass, a CSS file is generated. But what if you want that CSS file to be in a slightly different format? We have a few options to choose from. This means you can have your CSS output in a style that *you* prefer.

In the command line, you can type this:

```
sass --style
```

Follow this with the name of the style you want. The four options we have are called nested, expanded, compact, and compressed.

Nested is the default output style. It looks very much like regular CSS, with curly braces and semicolons.

Expanded is, as its name suggests, an expanded form of the CSS output. All classes—including nested ones—expand rather than remaining nested in their parents. Both nested and expanded styles are probably the easiest to read, but they also have the largest file sizes.

Compact puts all the properties of a selector on one line so it's easier to scan down a list of selectors.

Finally, compressed is possibly the most difficult to read. All spaces are removed, so the CSS sits on one line. This makes a compressed CSS file the smallest, which is great for mobile devices, for example.

➤ Check out the Sass we'll be compiling in each case.

```
basics/outputs.scss
.infobox {
  .message {
    border: 1px solid red;
    background: #336699;
    .title {
      color: red; } } }
```

➤ Nested (the default setting) looks like this.

```
.infobox .message {
  border: 1px solid red;
  background: #336699; }
  .infobox .message .title {
    color: red; }
```

➤ Expanded looks like this.

```
.infobox .message {
  border: 1px solid red;
  background: #336699;
}
.infobox .message .title {
  color: red;
}
```

➤ Compact looks like this.

```
.infobox .message { border: 1px solid red;
                    background: #336699; }
.infobox .message .title { color: red; }
```

(The first declaration should be on one line.)

➤ Compressed looks like this.

```
.infobox .message{border:1px solid red;background:#336699}
    .infobox .message .title{color:red}
```

(The compressed output didn't fit on one line in the book, so we had to create another one. In the real thing, though, it is all on one line.)

9   Defining Variables

Have you ever been in a situation where you are copying the value of a color over and over again? That very specific blue that your clients want appears in so many places. Then, a couple of weeks later, they want you to change the color. Or—even worse—you have a whole lot of colors to change. Find and replace time! Color handling in CSS is not DRY (there's that *Don't Repeat Yourself* again!) at all.

Sass introduces variables to help us manage problems like this. All variables in Sass are prefixed with a $ sign. Assigning a variable looks a lot like typing in a CSS property. For instance, we can set the $primary_color variable by adding the super-simple line: $primary_color: #369;. That's it!

To use the variable, we can just use the variable name where we'd usually use the property value. If we had to change the colors of the whole document, all we'd need to do is change the hex value of the variable and it's sorted for us when the CSS compiles.

We can use variables to represent colors, sizes, percents, and several other things that are less commonly used. Anything that you can put to the right of a CSS property is easily understood by Sass.

Another neat thing about variables is they can be *global* or *scoped*. We've pretty much gone through global variables: They're when a variable is defined on its own line, and they apply to the whole style sheet. Scoped variables, on the other hand, appear within a selector and will only apply to that selector and its children.

We can set default variables with the !default tag after assignment. When a variable is used, the default is used if there are no other assignments to that variable.

It's pretty standard in a Sass document to declare the variables at the top of a file and use them throughout. If you're familiar with C, then you'll be familiar with using constants this way. Or if you have a large project, you might want to create a file that defines all of the variables. We'll show you how you can break up your Sass files in Task 12, *Importing*, on page 26.

➤ Define and use variables.

basics/variable_example.scss

```scss
$primary_color: #369;
$secondary_color: #eee;
$page_width: 300px;

body {
  // Set the background to be #369
  background: $primary_color;
  #wrapper {
    width: $page_width;
    background: white;
    border: $secondary_color;
    h1 {
      color: $primary_color; } } }
```

This compiles to:

```css
body {
  background: #336699; }
  body #wrapper {
    width: 300px;
    background: white;
    border: #eeeeee; }
    body #wrapper h1 {
      color: #336699; }
```

Related Tasks:

• Task 10, *Calculating a Layout*, on page 22
• Task 12, *Importing*, on page 26

10 Calculating a Layout

Sass allows you to do calculations on the fly and in your document: you can easily type width: 12px * 0.5; in your code!

…

OK, OK—we admit that's not terribly useful. But it is once we throw variables into the mix. Once we've defined a variable, Sass allows us to perform basic operations on that variable using standard operators for adding, subtracting, multiplying, and dividing (+, -, *, and /). The operators will be familiar to anyone who has done any amount of programming before.

We could say something like width: $page_width * 0.1 as a way to avoid hard-coding pixel values. When the CSS is compiled, this will be pre-calculated and will print out an exact width in pixels.

We can now do previously laborious tasks like calculating and maintaining proportions throughout a layout.

For example, we can define the width of the content area of the page as 500px. Then we can base the width of the sidebar as a proportion of the total width—say 0.2. If we wanted to change the size of the content area, the sidebar can automatically resize itself to fit. All it takes is variables plus some operator know-how.

A quick note about units here. If we define $page_width as *10em* and we multiply it by two, the resulting value will keep the em unit. The same goes if it were px. If you mix units, Sass will try to make them work, but if they are incompatible, Sass will display an error. For instance, you can't multiply a px value by a em value. It just doesn't make sense.

➤ Add, subtract, multiply, or divide using the standard operators.

```
basics/layout_calc.scss
$width: 10px;
$double_width: $width * 2;
$half_width: $width / 2;
$width_plus_2: $width + 2;
$width_minus_2: $width - 2;
```

➤ Use calculations inline.

```
basics/calc_inline.scss
$width: 500px;
$sidebar_percent: 0.2;
#page {
  width: $width;
  #sidebar {
    width: $width * $sidebar_percent; }
  #content {
    width: $width * (1 - $sidebar_percent); } }
```

This compiles to:

```
#page {
  width: 500px; }
  #page #sidebar {
    width: 100px; }
  #page #content {
    width: 400px; }
```

Related Tasks:

• Task 9, *Defining Variables,* on page 20

11   Creating Themes with Advanced Colors

Altering a color palette is always a pain. If we want a less saturated color, we go to the hex charts, find a color that is lighter or darker, then replace our original hex code with that. Let's say we have a background with the color #336699, and we want to make some text a little bit lighter (or a bit more saturated). We stab around in the dark until we find a suitable shade.

Sass makes this conversion a lot easier with a few neat functions. We've got lighten and darken, saturate and desaturate, and there's a whole bunch more in Appendix 1, *SassScript Function Reference*, on page 93. Just put the function before the color you wish to change.

But this doesn't just work for straightforward colors—we can also use it for color-based variables, darkening your $main_color, for example.

Using these functions and the ones in the examples opposite, it's easy to change the whole website from blue to pink, retaining any of the differences in saturation and lightness.

➤ Lighten/Darken colors.

```
#page {
  color: lighten(#336699, 20%); }
```

This compiles to:

```
#page {
  color: #6699cc; }
```

➤ Saturate/Desaturate colors.

```
$main_color: #336699;
#page {
  color: saturate($main_color, 30%); }
```

This compiles to:

```
#page {
  color: #1466b8; }
```

➤ Change the hue.

We use the adjust-hue function, followed by the number of degrees we want to rotate the hue.

```
$main_color: #336699;
#page {
  color: adjust-hue($main_color, 180); }
#page {
  color: adjust-hue(desaturate($main_color, 10%), 90); }
```

➤ Desaturate by 100 percent with grayscale.

```
grayscale(#336699);
```

Using this method is the same as typing this:

```
desaturate(#336699, 100%);
```

➤ Mix colors.

This function allows you to mix colors as best as we can guess.

```
#page {
  color: mix(#336699, #993266); }
```

Mixing blue and red gives a beautiful purple:

```
color: #664c7f;
```

12 Importing

When you're developing, it's often useful to have many smaller style sheets rather than one huge one. This can be a pain for web performance. If you have five style sheets on a particular page, it can make the page loading times much slower because each style sheet needs a separate request to load.

Importing is a process by which a lot of files are turned into a few files. Sass has a neat little trick whereby the smaller style sheets are imported into the larger one as it is compiled into CSS. All you need to type is @import, followed by the name of the Sass file you want to import. You can mix Original Sass and SCSS at will with imports—it's all the same. Just say @import "sub_page"; and you're done!

If you don't want a Sass file to generate a corresponding CSS file, just start the filename with an underscore (if you're familiar with Rails, this is a bit like doing a Rails partial). For example, you can name the file _sub_page.sass. In the import line, you can leave off the underscore. If you don't mind that a separate style sheet is created for the child page, it can just be named sub_page.sass.

It's as simple as that. Any variables or *mixins* (we'll get to those later) you used in the imported style sheet can be used in the parent file too.

➤ Create a separate file.

```
basics/_colors.scss
$main_color: #336699;

// A LOT MORE COLORS GO HERE.
```

```
basics/widths.scss
$main_width: 720px;

// A LOT MORE WIDTHS GO HERE.
```

➤ Import into the main file.

```
@import "colors";
@import "widths";
```

(We don't need to include the underscore or extension with _colors.scss.)

```
basics/bundling_example.scss
@import "colors";
@import "widths";

#page {
  color: $main_color;
  width: $main_width; }

#sidebar {
  color: darken($main_color, 10%);
  width: $main_width*0.2; }
```

This compiles to:

```
#page {
  color: #336699;
  width: 720px; }

#sidebar {
  color: #264c73;
  width: 144px; }
```

Remember the rule about the underscores—when we compile into CSS, the two imported files will not be treated the same. The widths.scss file will create its own separate CSS file because it doesn't start with an underscore.

Related Tasks:

- Task 13, *Building a Font Family Library*, on page 28
- Task 14, *Resetting CSS*, on page 30
- Task 16, *Keeping Code Clean with Mixins*, on page 38

13 Building a Font Family Library

In regular CSS, we specify fonts like this:

```
font-family: "helvetica neue", arial, helvetica, freesans,
             "liberation sans", "numbus sans l", sans-serif;
```

We have to list all our preferred fonts in the order we want them. Then, inevitably, we have to include the most basic serif or sans serif at the end—just in case none of our fonts are available. But if we want to switch between fonts on a page, then we have to copy and paste this list over and over in different places or use ugly, nonsemantic font classes. So much repeated code. We've got a simpler way.

We can use variables in Sass! Instead of typing out the list of fonts over and over, define a variable at the top of the page. Then, when you want to add that long string of font names to a selector, just use the variable the way you normally would.

So much easier, don't you agree? But we can make it even easier. In almost every one of our projects, we have a set of font-variables that we always include, which we've shown on the opposite page.

You can put this at the beginning of your style sheets. Or, to keep your style sheets cleaner, you could use the importing technique we've just seen. Make a separate style sheet with all the fonts in it called, for example, _fonts.sass. Then import the file (using @import) at the top of your main style sheet.

➤ Define a variable with your fonts.

```
$helvetica: "helvetica neue", arial, helvetica, freesans,
            "liberation sans", "numbus sans l", sans-serif;
```

➤ Use the font variable as usual.

```
body {
  font-family: $helvetica; }
```

➤ Try this simple font library.

basics/font_family.scss
```
$helvetica: "helvetica neue", arial, helvetica, freesans,
            "liberation sans", "numbus sans l", sans-serif;

$geneva:    geneva, tahoma, "dejavu sans condensed",
            sans-serif;

$lucida:    "lucida grande", "lucida sans unicode",
            "lucida sans", lucida, sans-serif;

$verdana:   verdana, "bitstream vera sans", "dejavu sans",
            "liberation sans", geneva, sans-serif;

$cambria:   cambria, georgia, "bitstream charter",
            "century schoolbook l", "liberation serif", times,
            serif;

$palatino:  "palatino linotype", palatino, palladio,
            "urw palladio l", "book antiqua",
            "liberation serif", times, serif;

$times:     times, "times new roman", "nimbus roman no9 l",
            freeserif, "liberation serif", serif;

$courier:   "courier new", courier, freemono, "nimbus mono l",
            "liberation mono", monospace;

$monaco:    monaco, "lucida console", "dejavu sans mono",
            "bitstream vera sans mono", "liberation mono",
            monospace;
```

Related Tasks:

• Task 9, *Defining Variables*, on page 20
• Task 12, *Importing*, on page 26

14 Resetting CSS

A common technique to reset a style sheet is to override all of the default styles that browsers provide before you begin styling a site. This way, you won't accidentally assume—for instance—that all <h1> tags are the same font and font size between browsers. The default <h1> is different in Internet Explorer, Firefox, Safari… it's so annoying! To get around this frustration, designers often employ a "reset CSS" file.

On the right, we've provided a Sass version of the most famous reset CSS file by Eric Meyer. It's slightly shorter than the original CSS version.

You probably don't want to add all that boilerplate to the top of your master style sheet, so it's often more useful to employ the importing technique. Put the reset file into a separate style sheet named something like _reset.scss. Then at the start of the style sheet, put the following: @import "reset"; and the reset is magically incorporated into the CSS file when it's compiled.

➤ Reset CSS.

```
basics/reset.scss
/*
    Sass Reset - Converted by Hampton Catlin
    A modification of the original found at...
    http://meyerweb.com/eric/tools/css/reset/
*/
html, body, div, span, applet, object, iframe, h1, h2, h3, h4,
h5, h6, p, blockquote, pre, a, abbr, acronym, address, big,
cite, code, del, dfn, em, img, ins, kbd, q, s, samp, small,
strike, strong, sub, sup, tt, var, b, u, i, center, dl, dt, dd,
ol, ul, li, fieldset, form, label, legend, table, caption,
tbody, tfoot, thead, tr, th, td, article, aside, canvas,
details, embed, figure, figcaption, footer, header, hgroup,
menu, nav, output, ruby, section, summary, time, mark, audio,
video {
  margin: 0;
  padding: 0;
  border: 0;
  font-size: 100%;
  font: inherit;
  vertical-align: baseline; }
/* HTML5 display-role reset for older browsers */
article, aside, details, figcaption, figure, footer,
header, hgroup, menu, nav, section {
  display: block; }
body {
  line-height: 1; }
ol, ul {
  list-style: none; }
blockquote, q {
  quotes: none; }
blockquote {
  &:before, &:after {
    content: '';
    content: none; } }
q {
  &:before, &:after {
    content: '';
    content: none; } }
table {
  border-collapse: collapse;
  border-spacing: 0; }
```

Related Tasks:

- Task 12, *Importing,* on page 26
- Task 26, *Resetting: Much Easier with Compass,* on page 64

Part II

Advanced

Now we've gone through the basics of Sass, let's move on to some of the more advanced features it offers:

- First off, we'll go through @extend, which helps clone attributes: Task 15, *Keeping It Semantic: @extend*, on page 36.

- Next, we've got Task 16, *Keeping Code Clean with Mixins*, on page 38, a useful way to keep your style sheets clean. We'll expand on mixins in the next task, Task 17, *Taking Mixins Further with Variables*, on page 40.

- Then we'll look at how to debug your Sass in Task 18, *Debugging*, on page 42.

- We'll see how you can simplify the Sass necessary to style for different browsers in Task 19, *Generating Cross-Browser Rounded Borders*, on page 44, and Task 20, *Using Cross-Browser Opacity*, on page 46.

- We'll learn how to dynamically generate your Sass code in Task 21, *Interpolating*, on page 48.

- Two more programmer-style functions are covered in Task 22, *Stop Repeating Yourself with @each*, on page 50, and Task 23, *Determining Conditions with @if*, on page 52. @each applies the same set of rules to a list, and @if allows conditions in your CSS.

- And finally, want to change CSS layout depending on what device your user is using? Check out Task 24, *Changing Looks with Nested @media*, on page 54.

15 Keeping It Semantic: @extend

Keeping things semantic is a philosophy where everything is named logically. We name items based on what they *do*, not what they look like. We don't want to name something .blue_button; we want to name it .checkout_button, which is far more useful when we're going through the code.

But what if you had a set of attributes—say a blue button—that needed to be applied to multiple buttons with different functions? You want to name the buttons after their function, but it would be a pain typing out the set of attributes over and over again.

This is where @extend comes in. @extend clones the attributes from one class or ID and adds them to another. Let's run with the example we had with the blue button. Say we want to use the blue button style for the checkout button. If we've defined the blue button class elsewhere, all we need to do is use @extend, followed by the .blue_button class in the declaration of your selector.

You'll notice that the CSS output has two selectors. What @extend does is merge all the properties and values from both selectors, with a list of selectors merged before the declaration block.

We can also tweak the style being copied. What if we needed the checkout button to be slightly darker than the regular blue button? We can just add those properties we need to change onto the end of the declaration block. The new attributes you add will override the old ones.

This saves us so much time when we're coding. There's far less copying and pasting: you'll barely ever use Ctrl+C again.

➤ Use @extend in a selector.

First we make sure we've described the class elsewhere:

```
advanced/atextend_blueButton.scss
.blue_button {
  background: #336699;
  font-weight: bold;
  color: white;
  padding: 5px; }
```

Then we can @extend the class to another:

```
advanced/atextend_use.scss
.checkout_button {
  @extend .blue_button }
```

This compiles to:

```
.blue_button, .checkout_button {
  background: #336699;
  font-weight: bold;
  color: white;
  padding: 5px; }
```

➤ Modify a selector.

```
advanced/atextend_use_modified.scss
.checkout_button {
  @extend .blue_button;
  color: darken(#336699, 10%); }
```

16 Keeping Code Clean with Mixins

Mixins are some of the more powerful elements of Sass. A mixin is a fragment of Sass that can easily be applied to another selector. Let's say we require a distinct style: blue text with small caps. We need to apply this style to many selectors in our document. We don't want to have to repeat color: #369; over and over again. This is the perfect situation for a mixin!

To define a mixin, all you need to type is @mixin, followed by the name of the mixin and then its styling.

Once we've defined it, we can easily use a mixin wherever we please—it's a super-portable set of attributes. When you want to use the mixin, just type @include.

Mixins also help us keep our code semantic. We can define a mixin as blue_text, then apply it to a class with a more specific name, such as product_title.

It's useful to have mixins in a separate style sheet, keeping your main style sheet cleaner. If this is the case, we need to use the bundling technique—put @import at the top of your main Sass file, linking in the mixins file.

Depending on whether you're using Original Sass or SCSS, the use of mixins is slightly different. We've been through the SCSS way, where we describe a mixin with @mixin and use it with @include. With Original Sass, we use = before the mixin description and use + instead of the @include command.

➤ Define a mixin.

advanced/mixin_text.scss
```
@mixin blue_text {
  color: #336699;
  font-family: helvetica, arial, sans-serif;
  font-size: 20px;
  font-variant: small-caps; }
```

➤ Use a mixin.

advanced/mixin_use.scss
```
.product_title {
  @include blue_text; }
```

This compiles to:

```
.product_title {
  color: #336699;
  font-family: helvetica, arial, sans-serif;
  font-size: 20px;
  font-variant: small-caps; }
```

➤ Use mixins in Original Sass style.

Define these:

advanced/mixin_useS.sass
```
=blue_text
  color: #336699
  font-family: helvetica, arial, sans-serif
  font-size: 20px
  font-variant: small-caps
```

And use this:

advanced/mixin_useS.sass
```
.product_title
  +blue_text
```

Related Tasks:

- Task 12, *Importing*, on page 26
- Task 17, *Taking Mixins Further with Variables*, on page 40

17 Taking Mixins Further with Variables

So far, the idea of a mixin is pretty similar to what we came across in @extend—a set of attributes we apply somewhere else. With @extend, however, all values must stay the same. Mixins are more complex.

Mixins can include arguments (i.e., descriptors) that allow you to *vary your values*. Take the mixin we defined in the last task—blue_text. It has a set of attributes associated with it. What if you want the text size to be variable? You can easily include this in the mixin. Instead of putting a predefined font size, put $size (or whatever you wish to call it). Then, when naming your mixin, include the $size part in parentheses after the name.

When you want to use the mixin, include the argument after the mixin like you would when using a regular function.

You can also have a default value associated with a mixin. Just add the value after the variable. If you don't specify a value when you're using your mixin, the default will be used. If you want to change it, just add the new value like you would for a regular variable.

➤ Define a mixin with variable attributes.

advanced/mixin_argument.scss
```
@mixin blue_text($size) {
  color: #336699;
  font-family: helvetica, arial, sans-serif;
  font-size: $size;
  font-variant: small-caps; }
```

➤ Add the value you want after the mixin.

advanced/mixin_argument_use.scss
```
.product_title {
  @include blue_text (15px); }
```

➤ Define a mixin with a default value.

advanced/mixin_default.scss
```
@mixin blue_text($size: 20px) {
  color: #336699;
  font-family: helvetica, arial, sans-serif;
  font-size: $size;
  font-variant: small-caps; }
```

➤ Use a mixin with and without the default.

advanced/mixin_default_use.scss
```
.product_title {
  @include blue_text; }

.product_title {
  @include blue_text (100px); }
```

This compiles to:

```
.product_title {
  color: #336699;
  font-family: helvetica, arial, sans-serif;
  font-size: 20px;
  font-variant: small-caps; }

.product_title {
  color: #336699;
  font-family: helvetica, arial, sans-serif;
  font-size: 100px;
  font-variant: small-caps; }
```

18 Debugging

What if there's a bug in our code? It happens to the best of us. We can generally say that there are two kinds of bugs we can encounter. One is a syntactical error made while writing the Sass—that is, we may have passed in the wrong number of arguments to a function. Luckily, Sass makes finding these mistakes a breeze. The Sass development team has worked really hard to make sure that the error messages make as much sense as possible.

On top of that, if you have an error in your Sass code, it won't just keep quiet. Sass *could* have failed silently, where you would reload the page you are styling and all of a sudden it would be unstyled. Sass doesn't play that way. Sass loves you! Sass will generate a special CSS style sheet that will actively print out the message on the page you are styling. It uses the fun CSS trick of using the body:before selector and the content= property to inject the error *right on the page*!

We also have ways to debug more complex issues. When generating the Sass, we can pass in *options* to help us out. The line-comments option causes every selector in the CSS file you create to have a reference to the file and line number where it came from. This is especially useful when you are importing many files and want to see where a particular rule is defined.

Another option available is debug-info, which produces a more browser-friendly version of the line-comments option. In particular, it works well with an add-on to Firefox called FireSass for Firebug.[7]

There are many different ways to run Sass—maybe with Rails or the command-line interface or an integrated development environment (IDE)—and each has its own specific way of setting Sass options. The references provided in the book should be a good starting place.

---

7. https://addons.mozilla.org/en-US/firefox/addon/firesass-for-firebug/

➤ Write some invalid Sass.

advanced/debug_error.scss
```
@import "notfound"
```

➤ See an error page!

If you include the resulting CSS file in a web page, you'll see this in your web browser when you load the page!

```
Syntax error: File to import not found or unreadable: notfound.
            Load paths:
                /Users/hcatlin/dev/hcsass/Book/code/advanced
                /Users/hcatlin/dev/hcsass/Book/code/advanced
        on line 1 of ./debug_error.scss

1: @import "notfound"
```

➤ Compile with the line-comments option.

```
$> sass --line-comments nesting.scss
/* line 2, nesting.scss */
.infobox .message {
  border: 1px solid red; }
  /* line 4, nesting.scss */
  .infobox .message .title {
    color: red; }
/* line 6, nesting.scss */
.infobox .user {
  border: 1px solid black; }
  /* line 8, nesting.scss */
  .infobox .user .title {
    color: black; }
```

19 Generating Cross-Browser Rounded Borders

Rounded borders are a complex thing. We need to use a different method of calculation for Internet Explorer, Firefox, and Webkit. Wouldn't it be so much easier if there were one simple way of doing it?

Why, you can have one simple way: with Sass! There's a mixin that allows you to define the rounded borders for all three main browsers. This keeps our code clean and we don't need to repeat ourselves.

Just so you know, many of these macros come preinstalled with Compass, which we'll look at more in Part III, *Compass*, on page 59.

➤ Use this mixin for rounded borders.

advanced/cross_browser_borders.scss

```scss
@mixin rounded_borders($color, $width: 5px, $rounding: 5px) {
  -moz-border-radius: $rounding $rounding;
  -webkit-border-radius: $rounding $rounding;
  -khtml-border-radius: $rounding $rounding;
  -o-border-radius: $rounding $rounding;
  border-radius: $rounding $rounding;
  border: $width $color solid; }
```

And you can include it like any regular mixin:

advanced/cross_browser_borders_use.scss

```scss
.header {
  @include rounded_borders(#336699, 3px) }
```

This compiles to:

```css
.header {
  -moz-border-radius: 5px 5px;
  -webkit-border-radius: 5px 5px;
  -khtml-border-radius: 5px 5px;
  -o-border-radius: 5px 5px;
  border-radius: 5px 5px;
  border: 3px #336699 solid; }
```

20 Using Cross-Browser Opacity

We saw how browsers can be awkward in the previous task, needing different ways to define rounded borders. However, the differences don't stop there. Changing the opacity of something is simple in Firefox, Safari, and Opera because of this handy function: opacity. Opacity in most browsers is defined from 1, meaning fully opaque, to 0, meaning completely invisible.

Life's never so simple, though. Internet Explorer requires us to use a different method—something called filter. It takes a value between 0 and 100 instead, in this style:

```
filter: alpha(opacity = 60);
```

Depending on how you view opacity, either the 0–1 or the 0–100 scale can be more logical. It's pretty easy to convert between the two.

➤ Change opacity across browsers (0–100 scale).

advanced/cross_browser_opacity.scss

```scss
@mixin opacity($opacity) {
  filter: alpha(opacity=#{$opacity}); // IE 5-9+
  opacity: $opacity * 0.01; }
```

advanced/cross_browser_opacity_use.scss

```scss
@import "cross_browser_opacity.scss";

.h1 {
  @include opacity(60); }
```

This compiles to:

```scss
.h1 {
  filter: alpha(opacity=60);
  opacity: 0.6; }
```

➤ Change this to a 0–1 scale, if necessary.

advanced/cross_browser_opacity_one.scss

```scss
@mixin opacity($opacity) {
  filter: alpha(opacity=#{$opacity*100}); // IE 5-9+
  opacity: $opacity; }
```

21   Interpolating

Included in Sass are some programmer-style functions, which we'll look over in the next couple of tasks. We generally refer to these as *SassScripts*.

Let's start out with a general SassScript that allows you to dynamically generate style sheets. It's called *interpolation*. Oh, fancy sounding word —how we love you! It makes us sound smart just by saying it. You try it: *interpolation*. Feels good, doesn't it? OK, sorry—we got a bit distracted there.

Interpolation basically means "put this there." Imagine we want to write a mixin that has a dynamic property or selector. And we don't mean a dynamic property value—that's easy stuff that we've already done. We mean if the very *name* of a property or selector could be dynamically generated. Well, you're in luck, because that's exactly what interpolation can do.

Just wrap the name of a variable in #{} and you are done. For example, we could have #{$myvar}. The variable will be printed out wherever you put that. So, we could say .red_#{$carname}. And, if $carname is set to volvo, it would generate the selector .red_volvo. Wha-bam! Victory!

You can pretty much use interpolation anywhere you want in your Sass files. Go crazy!

➤ Interpolate to create a dynamic selector.

```scss
advanced/interpolation.scss
@mixin car_make($car_make, $car_color) {
  // Set the $car_make with "_make" at the end as a class
  .car.#{$car_make}_make {
    color: $car_color;
    width: 100px;
    .image {
      background: url("images/#{$car_make}/#{$car_color}.png");
    }
  }
}

@include car_make("volvo",    "green");
@include car_make("corvette", "red"  );
@include car_make("bmw",      "black");
```

This compiles to:

```css
.car.volvo_make {
  color: "green";
  width: 100px; }
  .car.volvo_make .image {
    background: url("images/volvo/green.png"); }

.car.corvette_make {
  color: "red";
  width: 100px; }
  .car.corvette_make .image {
    background: url("images/corvette/red.png"); }

.car.bmw_make {
  color: "black";
  width: 100px; }
  .car.bmw_make .image {
    background: url("images/bmw/black.png"); }
```

Related Tasks:

• Task 22, *Stop Repeating Yourself with @each*, on page 50

22   Stop Repeating Yourself with @each

@each is a trick to keep your Sass DRY (the tenet of *Don't Repeat Yourself*). It's a way of copying the same style for a lot of different variables.

Say we have a bunch of pictures, all with similar file URLs. The file URLs can include figures or punctuation, if necessary. We want to use them in the same way in each case but with slightly different classes. Usually, we'd have to write out each selector separately, replacing a single word each time. So much time, effort, and copying/pasting! This is where @each comes to the rescue.

We follow @each with the name of the generic variable we want to use, then with all the members of the group that we want to apply this to. When compiling the CSS, the list forms automatically.

You'll notice in the code that we wrap the variable selector name in #{}, which we learned about in the previous task.

➤ Copy one style to many variables with @each.

```
advanced/ateach.scss
@each $member in thom, jonny, colin, phil {
  .#{$member}_picture {
    background-image: url("/image/#{$member}.jpg"); } }
```

This compiles to:

```
.thom_picture {
  background-image: url("/image/thom.jpg"); }

.jonny_picture {
  background-image: url("/image/jonny.jpg"); }

.colin_picture {
  background-image: url("/image/colin.jpg"); }

.phil_picture {
  background-image: url("/image/phil.jpg"); }
```

Related Tasks:

- Task 21, *Interpolating,* on page 48

23 Determining Conditions with @if

Similar to @each, there's another feature called @if that allows us to write conditions in our Sass. This kind of feature is mostly useful when writing what we generally refer to as *SassScript*, writing reusable mixins and functions for Sass.

Oftentimes when writing a mixin that should be used across projects, we want to react to some variable that is passed in. For instance, if you had a mixin called width, you might want to do nothing if the first argument passed in is less than 0. There are lots of situations where we might want our mixins to act smart and react to the values that we pass in.

After the @if keyword, we can put a *statement* that will evaluate to true or false. For example, 20 > 10 would evaluate to true. And, "hello" == "world" would evaluate to false. Other common comparators are available, such as == (equal to), != (not equal to), > (greater than), and < (less than).

If the statement is true, whatever is inside the following declaration block will be executed. If the statement is false, then it looks for an @else as the next block to continue trying until it successfully matches. If it runs out of @else blocks, then it doesn't do anything at all.

In our trite (and nationalistic) example, we have a country color mixin. We want a particular color to show up only for particular countries. So, we have @if at the start, and each following country gets an @else if. The first condition to be satisfied by the variable will be executed, and the following ones will stop.

➤ Build a mixin with @if.

```
advanced/atif.scss
@mixin country_color($country) {
  @if $country == france {
    color: blue; }
  @else if $country == spain {
    color: yellow; }
  @else if $country == italy {
    color: green; }
  @else {
    color: red; } }

.england {
  @include country_color(england); }
.france {
  @include country_color(france); }
```

This compiles to:

```
.england {
  color: red; }

.france {
  color: blue; }
```

24 Changing Looks with Nested @media

Sometimes we'd like to change what is displayed based on the device on which the content is being displayed. CSS2 introduced the concept of @media. Various attributes, such as *print, handheld,* or *tv* can be used to define different property values, such as font sizes, depending on the medium used to view the page.

The main flaw with @media is that it can't be nested. Say you want to have all the main areas in 15px font, except for when you print the document. In CSS, you'd have to copy out all the declarations again.

Sass to the rescue! We can just add in another declaration specifically for one type of media, and it's compiled into a whole new selector when the CSS style sheet is made.

This is particularly useful in the era of the mobile web. The *handheld* attribute should alter the page if it's being viewed on a handheld device. However, a lot of phones don't currently seem to support it. There's a neat trick around this: use a maximum screen width. We'll use the iPhone as an example.

We know that the maximum width of the iPhone screen in portrait mode is 320px. We can just add this on to the end of our @media! Using it in a nested style allows us to say that the font should be larger only when the screen is at a maximum of 320px wide. When this is the only change we need to make, it's SO much easier than having a whole separate selector.

Added bonus: for landscape, we choose a minimum width of 321px and a maximum width of 480px.

➤ Use @media in a nested style.

```
advanced/atmedia.scss
.main {
  color: #336699;
  font-size: 15px;
  @media print {
  font-size: 10px; } }
```

This compiles to:

```
.main {
  color: #336699;
  font-size: 15px; }
  @media print {
    .main {
      font-size: 10px; } }
```

➤ Make your sites portrait-specific...

```
advanced/atmedia_phone_portrait.scss
.main {
  color: #336699;
  font-size: 15px;
  @media screen and (max-width: 320px) {
    font-size: 35px; } }
```

➤ ...or landscape-specific.

```
advanced/atmedia_phone_landscape.scss
.main {
  color: #336699;
  font-size: 15px;
  @media screen and (min-width: 321px) and (max-width: 480px) {
    font-size: 25px; } }
```

Part III

Compass

Compass is a library of mixins, functions, and other useful extensions to Sass. Chris Eppstein created Compass and maintains it to this day. Compass is a toolkit that any Sass-master should have handy. Because of its value in Sass development, we've devoted a whole chapter to some of its features—but it's a mere sampling of what Compass has to offer. Check out the Compass website for more.[8]

Make sure RubyGems is up-to-date, then install the Compass gem.

```
gem update --system
gem install compass
```

Then, compile your style sheets with --compass.

```
sass --compass myfile.scss myfile.css
sass --compass --watch .
```

Here's a summary of what we'll look at in this part.

---

8. http://compass-style.org/reference/compass/

- We'll expand items to fit inside a box in Task 32, *Stretching Elements*, on page 76.

- Want a much simpler, more concise way of creating tables? You can find the solution in Task 33, *Jazzing Up Layouts with Columns*, on page 78.

- And finally, we'll look at converting separate images into one big image in Task 34, *Spriting*, on page 80.

25 Setting Up for a Compass Project

In the introduction to this part, we saw the simple method for using Compass via the sass --compass command. However, if you want to do more advanced things in Compass, you can set up a Compass project. If you are familiar with Rails or Drupal or other similar frameworks, you'll be familiar with this kind of process. Compass sets up default files and folders for you to work with.

If you use another framework like Rails with Sass, you should reference how to set up a Compass project for it. If you are just using the command line (which we recommend for following along with this book), then we recommend using the method detailed on the next page.

Once you have generated your project, you can place your Sass files in the sass/ folder. If you want to change any Compass settings, feel free to edit the config.rb file. Compiled CSS is placed inside the css/ folder.

To compile a project, simply run compass compile. If you want to watch the whole project for changes, then use compass watch.

➤ Create a project.

This only works if you followed the compass gem install instructions found at the introduction to this part.

```
$> compass create my_project_name
```

This should print out the following:

```
directory my_project_name/sass/
directory my_project_name/style sheets/
   create my_project_name/config.rb
   create my_project_name/sass/screen.scss
   create my_project_name/sass/print.scss
   create my_project_name/sass/ie.scss
   create my_project_name/style sheets/ie.css
   create my_project_name/style sheets/print.css
   create my_project_name/style sheets/screen.css

*********************************************************
Congratulations! Your compass project has been created.
```

➤ Compile the project.

```
$> compass compile my_project_name
```

This should print out the following:

```
unchanged project/sass/ie.scss
unchanged project/sass/print.scss
unchanged project/sass/screen.scss
```

Obviously, if you changed the files, then they would get recompiled. Try that now!

26 Resetting: Much Easier with Compass

Compass comes with a really handy and super-robust reset style sheet built in. The advantage of using it is that it is far more complete than Eric Meyer's original reset CSS—and it includes a lot more browser tweaks. Plus, since Compass is a collection of libraries, we don't actually have to keep a file around anymore. This keeps our code a lot cleaner.

There are two types of reset. The first is *global reset*, which resets *all* the CSS. All you have to type is @import "compass/reset";. Most imports in Compass don't actually cause any styles to get printed in your style sheet, but this is a special case and it happens automatically. The CSS rendered is pretty much the same as the one we previously saw in Task 14, *Resetting CSS*, on page 30.

But say you don't want to reset *all* the CSS. Compass can help! Compass has several different reset mixins that you can use in your project if you only want to reset certain parts of the page. This is called a *nested reset*. Look on the opposite page for an example of a nested reset.[9]

---

9. See http://compass-style.org/reference/compass/reset/utilities/ for a complete refer-
    ence, as we've only provided a couple of examples of different built-in reset
    mixins.

➤ Reset everything with this excruciatingly simple import.

```
@import "compass/reset";
```

➤ Reset only *some* bits of the page like this.

compass/reset.scss
```
@import "compass/reset/utilities";

body {
  .sidebar {
    @include nested-reset; } }
```

This compiles to:

```
body .sidebar div, body .sidebar span, body .sidebar ...
body .sidebar h1, body .sidebar h2, body .sidebar h3, body ...
body .sidebar a, body .sidebar abbr, body .sidebar acronym, ...
body .sidebar del, body .sidebar dfn, body .sidebar em, ...
body .sidebar small, body .sidebar strike, body .sidebar ...
body .sidebar b, body .sidebar u, body .sidebar i, body ...
body .sidebar dl, body .sidebar dt, body .sidebar dd, body ...
body .sidebar fieldset, body .sidebar form, body .sidebar ...
body .sidebar table, body .sidebar caption, body .sidebar ...
body .sidebar article, body .sidebar aside, body .sidebar ...
body .sidebar figure, body .sidebar figcaption, body ...
body .sidebar menu, body .sidebar nav, body .sidebar ...
body .sidebar time, body .sidebar mark, body .sidebar ... {
  margin: 0;
  padding: 0;
  border: 0;
  font-size: 100%;
  font: inherit;
  vertical-align: baseline; }
body .sidebar table {
  border-collapse: collapse;
  border-spacing: 0; }
body .sidebar caption, body .sidebar th, body .sidebar td {
  text-align: left;
  font-weight: normal;
  vertical-align: middle; }
body .sidebar q, body .sidebar blockquote {
  quotes: none; }
  body .sidebar q:before, body .sidebar q:after, body ... {
    content: "";
    content: none; }
body .sidebar a img {
  border: none; }
```

The ellipses signify lines of code that are too long for the page.

27 Sprucing Up Your Lists

Lists need not be dull, vertical things with a single bullet point per item. You can manipulate them no end! Maybe it annoys you that you can't get rid of those bullet points that come with every unordered list. No worries: Compass has a great mixin called no-bullets, which removes all the bullet points from a list you're making. Neat, eh? If you want to remove only one bullet point, just @includeno-bullet in the class.

I know some of you might be shouting, "But that's so easy!" Well, it can be. It's so much easier using Compass because of its cross-browser capabilities. No longer do you have to download every browser imaginable to test your code.

We can also use our own custom bullet point designs. Once we've imported the correct Compass file, it's merely a case of using the pretty-bullets mixin, followed by the reference to the image you want to use for the bullet.

If you need to define the size of the bullet, you can add the pixel dimensions of the image after the image name. You can also define the line height and the padding you want, too.[10]

In the HTML, make sure to apply the class to the <ul> tag so all the items in the list have the special bullets applied to them.

---

10.   http://compass-style.org/reference/compass/typography/lists/bullets/

➤ Make a list.

```
compass/project/sass/lists.scss
@import "compass/typography/lists/bullets";

.flowerbullet {
  @include pretty-bullets("star.png"); }
```

This compiles to:

```
.flowerbullet {
  margin-left: 0; }
  .flowerbullet li {
    padding-left: 14px;
    background: url('../../../../images/compass/
        star.png?1320353498') no-repeat -5.5px -2.5px;
    list-style-type: none; }
```

(The no-repeat ...; should be on the same line as the background property, but the line was too wide for the book.)

➤ See how the list looks in your browser.

⁕ Puppies are fun.

⁕ Puppies are nice to stroke.

⁕ Puppies are loyal.

Related Tasks:

• Task 28, *Making Lists Horizontal,* on page 68

28 Making Lists Horizontal

As well as removing bullets and using your own icons, Compass gives you the cross-browser ease of making horizontal lists.

Horizontal lists are really useful for menus across the top of a page. They allow for easy navigation of a site.

You can also customize the padding between list points. Just type the padding you want after the horizontal list mixin. Pretty simple, no? Check out the Compass documentation for a couple of other things you can alter about lists.[11]

---

11. http://compass-style.org/reference/compass/typography/lists/horizontal_list/

➤ Add in the horizontal mixin.

compass/horlist.scss
```
@import "compass/typography/lists/horizontal-list";

ul.horiz {
  @include horizontal-list; }
```

This compiles to:

```
ul.horiz {
  margin: 0;
  padding: 0;
  border: 0;
  overflow: hidden;
  *zoom: 1; }
  ul.horiz li {
    list-style-image: none;
    list-style-type: none;
    margin-left: 0px;
    white-space: nowrap;
    display: inline;
    float: left;
    padding-left: 4px;
    padding-right: 4px; }
    ul.horiz li:first-child, ul.horiz li.first {
      padding-left: 0; }
    ul.horiz li:last-child {
      padding-right: 0; }
    ul.horiz li.last {
      padding-right: 0; }
```

➤ See how a horizontal list looks.

France Spain Italy UK

➤ Customize padding.

```
ul.horiz {
  @include horizontal-list(25px); }
```

Related Tasks:

• Task 27, *Sprucing Up Your Lists,* on page 66

29   Sticking a Footer to a Window

Sticky footers are, as the name suggests, footers that stick to the bottom of your browser. They're such a hassle to design in CSS. But in Compass there's a built-in mixin that allows you to make a sticky footer very simply.[12] All you need to define is the height (measured from the bottom of the page) at which the sticky footer floats.

There are three predefined selectors that we apply in this mixin: root, root_footer, and footer. We chose these three because they've already been built into Compass. You can see how we use them on the opposite page.

But hey, if you desperately want to use your own selector names, you can! For example, you can change the first ID, root, to a_root in the HTML. In your style sheet, specify this change by typing "#a_root" after you've defined the height of your footer in the @include function.

---

12. http://compass-style.org/reference/compass/layout/sticky_footer/

➤ Use sticky footers in the style sheet.

```
@import "compass/layout/sticky-footer"
```

Then using it is just a matter of this:

```
@include sticky-footer(24px)
```

➤ The built-in HTML for sticky footers is this.

compass/sticky_footer.html
```
<body>
  <div id="root">
    <div id="root_footer"></div>
  </div>
  <div id="footer">
    This is my footer!
  </div>
</body>
```

➤ Customize your sticky footer selectors.

Here's the HTML:

compass/sticky_footer_custom.html
```
<body>
  <div id="a_root">
    <div id="b_root_footer"></div>
  </div>
  <div id="c_footer">
    This is my footer!
  </div>
</body>
```

And here it is in use in the style sheet:

```
@include sticky-footer(24px, "#a_root", "#b_root_footer",
                                        "#c_footer")
```

30   Stopping Overflow with Clearfix

If you've been doing this as long as we have, you've definitely found out about the annoying little problems you can face with stretching divs to containers. Say you have an outer box with an undefined height and an inner box with a height of 100px. The outer box will not automatically stretch to also include the inner box, leaving an ugly overhang.

The Clearfix trick in Compass solves this problem. It makes sure that there's no overhang if your outer box isn't defined to be as tall as your inner box. It's a great way to solve some messy issues you're having with design.

➤ Start with this HTML.

compass/clearfix.html
```html
<div id="outer_box">
  <div id="inner_box"><p>Inner Box</p></div>
  <p>I'm in the outer box</p> </div>
```

➤ Use simple Sass.

compass/clearfix_original.scss
```scss
#outer_box {
  width: 500px;
  border: 4px solid black;
  #inner_box {
    float: left;
    width: 200px;
    height: 100px;
    background: gray; } }
```

➤ Take a look in your browser.

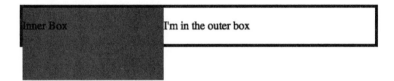

➤ Use Compass to save the day.

compass/clearfix.scss
```scss
@import "compass/utilities/general/clearfix";

#outer_box {
  @include clearfix;
  width: 500px;
  border: 4px solid black;
  #inner_box {
    float: left;
    width: 200px;
    height: 100px;
    background: gray; } }
```

➤ Take another look: Magically fixed!

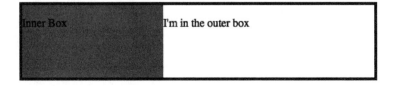

31   Truncating Text Using Ellipses

Say we have a large paragraph of text that overruns its bounds. Or maybe we just don't want to display the whole thing. There's a neat way, using Compass, to remove the extra text and replace it with an ellipsis (...).

First, you need to install some small compass components using the compass command-line interface. After that, use the @includeellipsis command just like any other Compass mixin.

But...there's a problem. This doesn't work for all browsers. It works for Chrome, Safari, and early versions of Internet Explorer, but not for Opera or Firefox. Firefox claims support is coming in the future, but apparently this feature has been pending for a long time.[13]

---

13. You can read more about this technique at http://mattsnider.com/css/css-string-truncation-with-ellipsis/.

➤ Install the ellipsis file on the command line.

```
compass install compass/ellipsis
```

➤ Use the mixin in SCSS.

```
compass/ellipses.scss
@import "compass/typography/text/ellipsis";
.dotdotdot {
  @include ellipsis;
  width: 500px; }
```

This compiles to:

```
.dotdotdot {
  white-space: nowrap;
  overflow: hidden;
  -o-text-overflow: ellipsis;
  -ms-text-overflow: ellipsis;
  text-overflow: ellipsis;
  width: 500px; }
```

➤ See how it looks in Safari.

This is a super-long block of text that's extremely dull, and no one in ...

32 Stretching Elements

One of the handy mixins in Compass is used for stretching. Its purpose is pretty straightforward: it allows you to stretch an element to fit into a box.

We need to define the space into which the element will be stretched, which is what we do when we're defining the stretch_box class. We also need something to stretch; in this case we're going to use the blue button from Task 15, *Keeping It Semantic: @extend*, on page 36.

At the top of your style sheet, you need to @import three stretching compass files: compass/layout/stretching, compass/utilities and compass/css3. Then all you need to do is @include the mixin wherever you need a class or ID to be stretched. A useful feature is that you can define an offset border, so that when you stretch an element, it won't completely reach the edge of your container box.

You can also stretch the element in either the *x*-axis (horizontally) or *y*-axis (vertically) only.

➤ Define a box and an element to be stretched.

compass/stretch.scss
```scss
.stretch_box {
  border: 2px solid black;
  width: 240px;
  height: 240px;
  position: relative;
  @include inline-block; }
```

➤ Stretch the button fully to all sides.

compass/stretch.scss
```scss
.stretched_fully {
  @extend .blue_button;
  @include stretch; }
```

➤ Include an offset to the stretch.

compass/stretch.scss
```scss
.stretched_with_gap {
  @extend .blue_button;
  @include stretch(12px, 12px, 12px, 12px); }
```

➤ Stretch only in the *x*- or *y*-axis.

compass/stretch.scss
```scss
.stretched_horizontally {
  @extend .blue_button;
  @include stretch-x; }
```

Appropriately, if you want to stretch it vertically, just use stretch-y instead.

➤ Use this HTML.

```html
<div class="stretch_box">
  <div class="stretched_fully">
    Stretched fully!
  </div>
</div>
```

➤ See how it looks in your browser.

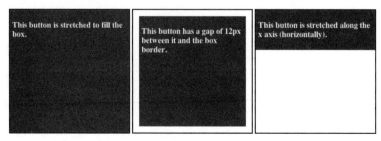

33 Jazzing Up Layouts with Columns

Say we want to make our website look more like a newspaper. We want to turn our boring one-column paragraph into multiple columns. This is a lot easier with Compass.

We have the option to apply any number of columns. We can use two extra mixins to define the width of each column as well as the gap between each column.

If necessary, we can add a line to separate the columns of text. The declarations we use are the same as what we would use for describing a regular border, namely the width, style, and color.

It's important to note that columns aren't really supported in older versions of Internet Explorer. Also, the column attribute doesn't really like it if you define heights.

➤ Turn text into columned text.

```
compass/columns.scss
#two_columns {
  @include column-count(2);
  width: 300px; }
```

➤ Define the width of columns and the gap between columns.

```
@include column-width(240px);
@include column-gap(24px);
```

➤ Add a border between the columns.

```
compass/columns.scss
#columns_borders {
  @include column-count (3);
  @include column-rule(2px, dashed, #336699);
  width: 300px; }
```

➤ See how these look in the browser.

This is an example
of a slightly long
block of text that
can be split into two
columns for the
purpose of this
example.

This is an : will have : rendered in
example of : borders : my
an even : between its : example.
longer block : columns :
of text that : when it is :

Related Tasks:

• Task 35, *Producing More Two-Column Layouts,* on page 86

34 Spriting

Spriting is a process by which many small icons or pictures are turned into one larger one for use in a website. The one larger file is *not* the direct sum of its parts—its file size is a lot smaller than the separate images combined. This is of supreme importance in the age of the mobile web, where every KB counts.

Creating a sprite image file for incorporation into your site is incredibly simple with Compass. We used to have to stitch together all the images using Photoshop and then define each image by its location in pixels. Compass does this all automatically for us.

We have to make sure all our images are in one folder—for example, icons. Then we @import the icons from the folder.

Compass makes the link.png, movie.png, and script.png icons into one big image. The sum of the three images is 876B, but the sprited image is only 357B—a huge savings! Compass gives the big image a unique identifier, which is why the file name will be something like icon-s2c4d35777d.png.

Once that's been sorted, you can specify a class (for example .movie_icon) and @include your image file name—in this case, movie. Compass compiles this, and in the CSS it defines a specific place in the image where our movie icon starts.

In the HTML, all you need to do is use the newly defined movie_icon class like you would any other class.

➤ Import sprites from an icon folder in Compass.

```
@import "icon/*.png";
```

➤ Compass combines three images into one.

➤ Specify a class with the necessary icon.

```
compass/project/sass/screen.scss
.movie_icon {
  height: 20px;
  @include icon-sprite(movie); }
```

This compiles to:

```
.icon-sprite, .movie_icon {
  background: url('../../../../images/compass/icon-s2c4d3.png')
              no-repeat;
}

/* line 8, ../sass/screen.scss */
.movie_icon {
  height: 20px;
  background-position: 0 -22px;
}
```

➤ Use in HTML.

```
<div class="movie_icon">
</div>
```

Part IV

Blueprint CSS

Remember how we used Compass to shortcut some cross-browser issues? Compass also helped with mixins for various tasks, such as shortening text or making a list a bit more exciting.

Blueprint is a framework that goes one step further than Compass—it's an even more extensive set of mixins that allows you to easily design your own site. Blueprint has many more predefined classes that you use when building a site. Take the caps class that we'll come across in Task 36, *Using Predefined Fancy Fonts*, on page 88. All we need to know is the class name, and Blueprint will sort out all the styling aspects of it for us.

The Blueprint website has a downloadable file containing Blueprint.[14] We're only covering a few aspects of Blueprint, but you can find a wiki and discussion forums on the site, where you can ask for help if necessary.

Here's a summary of what we're going to look at using Blueprint.

- Remember when we looked at how to make columns of text in Compass (Task 33, *Jazzing Up Layouts with Columns*, on page 78)? Well, we can do it another way using Blueprint. To see how, check out Task 35, *Producing More Two-Column Layouts*, on page 86.

- Then we'll look at some predefined font styles that come with Blueprint in Task 36, *Using Predefined Fancy Fonts*, on page 88.

- Finally, we'll look at ways to improve button aesthetics in Task 37, *Making Beautiful Buttons*, on page 90.

---

14. http://www.blueprintcss.org/

35   Producing More Two-Column Layouts

As we saw in Task 33, *Jazzing Up Layouts with Columns*, on page 78, we can use Compass to generate columns in our HTML. However, with Blueprint, there's an even easier way. Blueprint controls more of the column layout than Compass, but it still lets you have a say over the widths.

First we need to define the number of columns and the width of each column. Here we're using six columns of 65px width. Once we've done that, we can @import "blueprint".

As we start adding to the .two-col class, we must first include the container. We can also set the background and set other box-wide things here. Then it's on to the columns.

With our header, we want it to span the whole width of the item, and the same goes for the footer. So we'll apply the whole six columns to this bit using @include column(6).

For the links column and the main text area, we need to divide up the six columns between them—say two columns' worth for the links and the remaining four columns' worth for the main text. Simply add the number of columns you want each section to have to the @include column.

We need to add *true* to any column (or column set) that appears after another—this ensures the next column follows on from the previous column.

➤ Define the number and width of columns, then import Blueprint.

```
$blueprint_grid_columns: 6;
$blueprint_grid_width: 65px;

@import "blueprint";
```

➤ Columnize your text!

```
blueprint/twocolumn.scss
.two-col {
  @include container;
  background-color: #9ab3cc;
  #header, #footer {
    @include column(6); }
  #links {
    @include column(2); }
  #main_text {
    @include column(4, true); } }
```

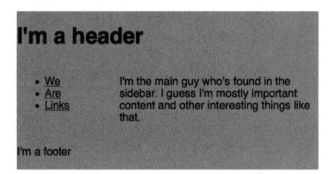

Related Tasks:

• Task 33, *Jazzing Up Layouts with Columns*, on page 78

36 Using Predefined Fancy Fonts

Blueprint has a couple of text modifying features built in. These allow you to quickly and easily modify text using predefined classes.

If we go through them in the order they're compiled to in the CSS, the first is the p + p element. The + symbol here is for styling something that follows something else—that is, the directions only apply to a paragraph that directly follows a paragraph. In this case, they indent the next paragraph rather than having a line space.

The incr class is used to space out lines as well as to make the font slightly smaller. We could use it if we wanted to make the text a bit smaller, for example, in a sidebar.

We can use the caps class as a kind of emphasizer, although it's not too easy to read long stretches of text.

Finally, there's the alt class, which makes your text italic and therefore look more handwritten. This is the fanciest one of all.

➤ Add the mixin into your style sheet.

blueprint/fancytype.scss

```scss
@import "blueprint/fancy-type";
body {
  @include fancy-type; }
```

This compiles to:

```css
@charset "utf-8";
body p + p {
  text-indent: 2em;
  margin-top: -1.5em; }
  form body p + p {
    text-indent: 0; }
body p.incr,
body .incr p {
  font-size: 0.833em;
  line-height: 1.44em;
  margin-bottom: 1.5em; }
body .caps {
  font-variant: small-caps;
  letter-spacing: 1px;
  text-transform: lowercase;
  font-size: 1.2em;
  line-height: 1%;
  font-weight: bold;
  padding: 0 2px; }
body .dquo {
  margin-left: -0.5em; }
body .alt {
  color: #666666;
  font-family: "Warnock Pro", "Goudy Old Style", "Palatino"...
  font-style: italic;
  font-weight: normal; }
```

➤ See how some of the classes look in your browser.

Ooh la la. I'm using the alt class!

I'M STERN 'COS I'M USING THE CAPS CLASS.

New paragraphs usually start a new line:
    They don't indent like this.
    But thanks to the p + p feature
    In Blueprint, they do!

37   Making Beautiful Buttons

If we use a semantic <button> tag, Blueprint makes it easy to style that button with a custom look. Just use the tag in your HTML as you normally would, import the required components (see the opposite page for an exact listing), and finally @includebutton-button. Once we've included that code, we are ready to style the <button> tags.[15]

As a best practice, if you are doing general styling of all buttons on the site, we recommend doing that in a separate file that you can include. This helps to keep the code more organized. We prefer to use a filename like _button_style.scss.

What if you want to make an <a> look like a button? This is a very common thing to do on the Web. Blueprint makes this easy, too!

First, @include the anchor-button, and then apply it to the anchor button class. When including the anchor button, you can alter the float of the button by typing *left* or *right* after anchor-button.

As for coloring options, there are four colors that you can play with in the design: the font color, the background color, the border color, and the border highlight color. (By default, the border highlight color is automatically set to one shade lighter than the border color.)

---

15. If you reference the Compass documentation at http://compass-style.org/reference/blueprint/buttons/, you'll see there are a boatload of variables you can use to style your buttons.

➤ Install Blueprint buttons.

```
compass install blueprint/buttons
```

➤ Style button tags.

```
@import "compass/utilities/general/float";
@import "blueprint/buttons";

button {
  @import button-button();
}
```

Wha-bam! There you go—magically all of the buttons are styled!

➤ Buttonize an anchor tag.

blueprint/buttons.scss
```
a.button {
  @include anchor-button; }
```

┌───┐
│ **I'm using the button class**   │
└───┘

➤ Change the color of a button.

blueprint/buttons.scss
```
a.button.positive {
  @include anchor-button(left);
  @include button-colors(#305d00, #b0dd80, #478c00);
  @include button-hover-colors(#305d00, #d8eec0, #84a560);}
```

Use the following HTML:

blueprint/buttons.html
```
<a class="button">
  I'm using the button class
</a>
<a class="button positive">
  I'm in a button!
</a>
<a class="button positive" id="hover">
  And I'm being hovered over
</a>
```

The result in the browser will look like this:

┌──────────────────┐ ┌──────────────────────────────┐
│ **I'm in a button!** │ │ **And I'm being hovered over** │
└──────────────────┘ └──────────────────────────────┘

SassScript Function Reference

rgb($red, $green, $blue)

Creates a {Color} object from red, green, and blue values.

hsl($hue, $saturation, $lightness)

Creates a {Color} object from hue, saturation, and lightness. Uses the algorithm from the CSS3 spec.[16]

hsla($hue, $saturation, $lightness, $alpha)

Creates a {Color} object from hue, saturation, and lightness, as well as an alpha channel indicating opacity. Uses the algorithm from the CSS3 spec.

red($color)

Returns the red component of a color.

green($color)

Returns the green component of a color.

blue($color)

Returns the blue component of a color.

hue($color)

Returns the hue component of a color.

See the CSS3 HSL specification.

---

16. http://www.w3.org/TR/css3-color/#hsl-color

Calculated from RGB where necessary via this algorithm.[17]

saturation($color)

Returns the saturation component of a color.

See the CSS3 HSL specification.

Calculated from RGB where necessary via the same algorithm as *hue($color)*.

lightness($color)

Returns the hue component of a color.

See the CSS3 HSL specification.

Calculated from RGB where necessary via the same algorithm as *hue($color)*.

alpha($*args)

Returns the alpha component (opacity) of a color. This is 1 unless otherwise specified.

This function also supports the proprietary Microsoft 'alpha(opacity=20)' syntax.

opacity($color)

Returns the alpha component (opacity) of a color. This is 1 unless otherwise specified.

opacify($color, $amount)

Makes a color more opaque. Takes a color and an amount between 0 and 1, and returns a color with the opacity increased by that value.

fade-in()

Makes a color more opaque. Takes a color and an amount between 0 and 1, and returns a color with the opacity increased by that value.

---

17. http://en.wikipedia.org/wiki/HSL_and_HSV#Conversion_from_RGB_to_HSL_or_HSV

transparentize($color, $amount)

Makes a color more transparent. Takes a color and an amount between 0 and 1, and returns a color with the opacity decreased by that value.

fade-out()

Makes a color more transparent. Takes a color and an amount between 0 and 1, and returns a color with the opacity decreased by that value.

lighten($color, $amount)

Makes a color lighter. Takes a color and an amount between 0% and 100%, and returns a color with the lightness increased by that value.

darken($color, $amount)

Makes a color darker. Takes a color and an amount between 0% and 100%, and returns a color with the lightness decreased by that value.

saturate($color, $amount)

Makes a color more saturated. Takes a color and an amount between 0% and 100%, and returns a color with the saturation increased by that value.

desaturate($color, $amount)

Makes a color less saturated. Takes a color and an amount between 0% and 100%, and returns a color with the saturation decreased by that value.

adjust-hue($color, $degrees)

Changes the hue of a color while retaining the lightness and saturation. Takes a color and a number of degrees (usually between -360deg and 360deg), and returns a color with the hue rotated by that value.

adjust-color($color, $kwargs)

Adjusts one or more properties of a color. This can change the red, green, blue, hue, saturation, value, and alpha properties. The properties are specified as keyword arguments and are added to or subtracted from the color's current value for that property.

'$red', '$green', and '$blue' properties should be between 0 and 255. '$saturation' and '$lightness' should be between 0% and 100%. '$alpha' should be between 0 and 1. All properties are optional.

You can't specify both RGB properties ('$red', '$green', '$blue') and HSL properties ('$hue', '$saturation', '$value') at the same time.

scale-color($color, $kwargs)

Scales one or more properties of a color by a percentage value. Unlike *adjust-color($color, $kwargs)*, which changes a color's properties by fixed amounts, scale_color fluidly changes them based on how high or low they already are. So if we use scale color twice: scale-color scale-color, it won't change the lightness much, but lightening a dark color by the same amount will change it more dramatically. This has the benefit of making 'scale-color($color, ...)' have a comparable effect across color palettes.

For example, the lightness of a color can be anywhere between 0 and 100. If 'scale-color($color, $lightness: 40%)' is called, the resulting color's lightness will be 40% of the way between its original lightness and 100. If 'scale-color($color, $lightness: -40%)' is called instead, the lightness will be 40% of the way between the original and 0.

This can change the red, green, blue, saturation, value, and alpha properties. The properties are specified as keyword arguments. All arguments should be percentages between 0% and 100%. All properties are optional.

You can't specify both RGB properties ('$red', '$green', '$blue') and HSL properties ('$saturation', '$value') at the same time.

change-color($color, $kwargs)

Changes one or more properties of a color. This can change the red, green, blue, hue, saturation, value, and alpha properties. The properties are specified as keyword arguments and replace the color's current value for that property.

'$red', '$green', and '$blue' properties should be between 0 and 255. '$saturation' and '$lightness' should be between 0% and 100%. '$alpha' should be between 0 and 1. All properties are optional.

You can't specify both RGB properties ('$red', '$green', '$blue') and HSL properties ('$hue', '$saturation', '$value') at the same time.

mix($color1, $color2, $weight = *50*)

Mixes together two colors. Specifically, takes the average of each of the RGB components, optionally weighted by the given percentage. The opacity of the colors is also considered when weighting the components.

The weight specifies the amount of the first color that should be included in the returned color. The default, 50%, means that half the first color and half the second color should be used. 25% means that a quarter of the first color and three quarters of the second color should be used.

grayscale($color)

Converts a color to grayscale. This is identical to 'desaturate(color, 100%)'.

complement($color)

Returns the complement of a color. This is identical to 'adjust-hue(color, 180deg)'.

invert($color)

Returns the inverse (negative) of a color. The red, green, and blue values are inverted, while the opacity is left alone.

unquote($string)

Removes quotes from a string if the string is quoted, or returns the same string if it's not.

quote($string)

Add quotes to a string if the string isn't quoted, or returns the same string if it is.

type-of($value)

Inspects the type of the argument, returning it as an unquoted string.

unit($number)

Inspects the unit of the number, returning it as a quoted string. Complex units are sorted in alphabetical order by numerator and denominator.

unitless($number)

Inspects the unit of the number, returning a boolean indicating if it is unitless.

comparable($number_1, $number_2)

Returns true if two numbers are similar enough to be added, subtracted, or compared.

percentage($value)

Converts a decimal number to a percentage.

round($value)

Rounds a number to the nearest whole number.

ceil($value)

Rounds a number up to the nearest whole number.

floor($value)

Rounds down to the nearest whole number.

abs($value)

Finds the absolute value of a number.

length($list)

Return the length of a list.

nth($list, $n)

Gets the nth item in a list.

Note that unlike some languages, the first item in a Sass list is number 1, the second is number 2, and so forth.

join($list1, $list2, $separator = "auto")

Joins together two lists into a new list.

Unless the '$separator' argument is passed, if one list is comma-separated and one is space-separated, the first parameter's separator is used for the resulting list. If the lists have only one item each, spaces are used for the resulting list.

append($list, $val, $separator = "auto")

Appends a single value onto the end of a list.

Unless the '$separator' argument is passed, if '$list' has only one item, the resulting list will be space-separated.

zip($*lists)

Combines several lists into a single comma-separated list, with spaces between similarly placed items. If we have the lists 1, 2, 3 and A, B, C, they will be combined into 1A, 2B, 3C, etc. The length of the resulting list is the length of the shortest list.

index($list, $value)

Returns the position of the given value within the given list. If not found, returns false.

if($condition, $if_true, $if_false)

Returns one of two values based on the truth value of the first argument.

numeric-transformation($value)

This method implements the pattern of transforming a numeric value into another numeric value with the same units. It yields a number to a block to perform the operation and return a different number.

Introduction to Haml

Haml is something of a sister language to Sass, but Haml was actually designed before Sass. It was successful enough that a CSS-version was developed, applying the same principles of Haml into CSS. They were both developed to clarify the meaning behind design.

Haml was created from the desire to write logically structured HTML that your designer would thank you for. HTML builders shouldn't make crap: the layout of the page and the information on the page should be logically structured and well named. Haml isn't a revolution; it's a statement of the obvious and an adoption of best practices.

Installing Haml is pretty similar to installing Sass. Once Ruby is installed, all you need to type in the command line is the following:

```
gem install haml
```

And you're done. It used to be that Haml was in the same gem as Sass, but since version 3.1 they've been split into two separate gems.

If you need any help with Haml, there's the Haml site and all its documentation,[18] which will have a lot more information than the snippet we've given here. In addition, there's a bunch of friendly people willing to help at the Haml Google group.[19]

---

18. http://haml-lang.com/ and http://haml-lang.com/docs/yardoc/ file.HAML_REFERENCE.html, respectively.
19. http://groups.google.com/group/haml

In this appendix, we've got two ways to take you through Haml. The first is from a Ruby-style angle, taking an example of ERB and reformatting it. The second is for those of us who are more familiar with HTML. They're both in a slightly different format to the rest of the book, as they follow the progression of ERB/HTML into Haml.

Haml Walkthrough: ERB

Now we're going to walk you through the exact same process with which Haml was created. A well-formatted bit of HTML was changed step-by-step until Haml was born.

Let's start with an example using ERB. It's a pretty standard template you might find in any Ruby project. Don't panic if you aren't a Rubyist—it's a straightforward example.

```
haml/haml_e1.html
<div id="products">
  <%- @products.each do |product| %>
    <div class="product" id="product_<%= product.id %>">
      <div class="name"><%= product.name %></div>
      <div class="price"><%= product.price %></div>
    </div>
  <% end %>
</div>
```

Executing this would print out each of the products in @products and assign each one a custom ID like product_23 (where the product's ID is 23). It's a very standard and well-formatted kind of template in ERB, and we are going to slowly convert this into Haml.

First off: it's important to correctly indent ERB files, so there is no reason why you should have to spend so much time closing tags—it just seems wasteful. So, we'll take the above example and remove all of the closing tags.

```
haml/haml_e2.html
<div id="products">
  <%- @products.each do |product| %>
    <div class="product" id="product_<%= product.id %>">
      <div class="name"><%= product.name %>
      <div class="price"><%= product.price %>
```

See how much cleaner it is? And notice that the <% end %> tag is gone too. Haml automatically figures out when to close a Ruby block. (This can vary in non-Ruby implementations.)

You're probably thinking we're secretly Python people because of the decision to make Haml "whitespace sensitive." That term's annoying. When looking at HTML, the advantages of getting rid of the closing tags were clear. Even when working in a language that doesn't care about whitespace, most people still do. Having bad indentation is a serious issue in any bit of code or markup and should be treated as a flaw.

Haml used to accept only two spaces as indentation—no exceptions. That has since changed. Whatever you use to start indenting is what you must keep with. Just stay consistent. It can be a tab, or one space, or two tabs. It doesn't matter. As long as it's consistent, it's OK.[20]

Moving on! We're not nearly done yet.

Don't you absolutely hate this line?

```
id="product_<%= product.id %>"
```

Ruby has a fantastic built-in string interpolation feature that means you should be able to do product_#{product.id} and skip all that weirdness. So let's do that.

```
haml/haml_e3.html
<div id="products">
 <%- @products.each do |product| %>
   <div class="product" id="product_#{product.id}">
     <div class="name"><%= product.name %>
     <div class="price"><%= product.price %>
```

There's only a small change this time, but already this example is far more readable. Always think about how readable something is at a glance. When you look at it, how quickly does your brain parse and understand what you're seeing? Basically, this removes a bunch of unneeded symbols for your eyes to deal with.

It's at this point that everyone's dislike of % style tags comes to full vengeance. Has anyone else done PHP for too many years and been left scarred and angry? Let's get rid of those!

---

20. However, we're still of the belief that using two spaces is far superior and should be used in Haml. We were convinced by an article by Jamie Zawinski that we strongly suggest you read: http://www.jwz.org/doc/tabs-vs-spaces.html

```
haml/haml_e4.html
<div id="products">
 - @products.each do |product|
   <div class="product" id="product_#{product.id}">
     <div class="name">
       = product.name
     <div class="price">
       = product.price
```

See, we kept the first character as - or = to signify nonprinting and printing lines. Anything after an = gets printed, and anything after a - is executed but its output ignored.

At this point in the transformation, printing lines have been moved down to their own line. We'll actually rectify this later, but for now it makes parsing the document a lot easier. Besides, <div>= seems inelegant for some reason.

In order to get those back up on the other line, Haml tags must be different from static HTML tags. One of the design goals is that you can copy in some plain HTML (properly indented) and it won't get too mad at you. Mostly this was a concern for the <meta> tags on a page, which no matter what you do are as ugly as sin.

So, let's use the % character to mean <tag> and use the Ruby/JSON-style syntax for the attributes. (Note: The JSON-style syntax only works with Ruby versions 1.9+. In 1.8, you must use the hashrocket style of {"class" => "product"}.)

```
haml/haml_e5.html
%div{id: "products"}
 - @products.each do |product|
   %div{class: "product" id: "product_#{product.id}"}
     %div{class: "name"}
       = product.name
     %div{class: "price"}
       = product.price
```

At this point, we have fully valid Haml. Congratulations! But we have a bit more to do. With this, we can now move those printing lines up again! It'll look nice.

```
haml/haml_e6.html
%div{id: "products"}
 - @products.each do |product|
   %div{class: "product" id: "product_#{product.id}"}
     %div{class: "name"}= product.name
     %div{class: "price"}= product.price
```

Now we are getting somewhere! But something is still not quite right. There is a lot of writing of class: and id:, and it requires the brain to read the letters to understand what it means. At this point, inspiration strikes. Can you think of a symbology that already exists for IDs and classes?

```
haml/haml_e7.html
%div#products
  - @products.each do |product|
    %div.product{id: "product_#{product.id}"}
      %div.name= product.name
      %div.price= product.price
```

Bam! Using CSS-style naming! We already know what those symbols mean. We're on a roll now!

In a larger example, there would be %div all over the place. And we still aren't encouraging the use of classes and IDs. It's a *lot* easier—a lot less typing to do the right thing.

What if we assumed that each tag was a <div> by default?

```
haml/haml_e8.html
#products
  - @products.each do |product|
    .product{id: "product_#{product.id}"}
      .name= product.name
      .price= product.price
```

Now that's nice! We only have to specify the name when it's not a div. And if we're lazy, it's easier to name divs well than it is to type %div over and over again. This is precisely how Haml should encourage good behavior. With this shortcut, it's actually hard to do the wrong thing and easier to do the right thing (i.e., name everything well!).

Now we've really arrived at some standard Haml. But there is one thing that is still troublesome—the whole id: "prod-uct_#{product.id}" line. It is a bit of an ugly duckling there.

If your object has a good answer for the object.id call, then we can automatically figure out the ID and class name that the .product div should have. We take the object's class and down-case it, add an underscore, then put in the obj.id value —all with this little shortcut.

```
haml/haml_e9.haml
#products
  - @products.each do |product|
```

```
%div[product]
  .name= product.name
  .price= product.price
```

The product div will automatically receive the proper class and ID, as in our products example. When we say [product] though, we're referring to the |product|variable. If we had named the variable in |product| as |x|, then it would be %div[x].

Haml Walkthrough: HTML

We're not going to go through the HTML to Haml conversion in as much detail as the previous ERB one. We just want to see how the stylistic changes can also be applied to a static site.

```
haml/haml_h1.html
<!DOCTYPE html PUBLIC "-//W3C//DTD XHTML 1.0
Transitional//EN" "http://www.w3.org/TR/xhtml1/DTD/
xhtml1-transitional.dtd">
<html xmlns="http://www.w3.org/1999/xhtml"
xml:lang="en">
  <head>
    <meta http-equiv="Content-Type" content="text/html;
charset=UTF-8" />
    <title><%= @title || "Awesome Site" %></title>
  </head>
  <body>
    <div id='wrapper'>
      <div id='header'>
        <h1>Awesome Site</h1>
      </div>
      <div id='content'>
        <%= yield %>
      </div>
      <div id='footer'>
        <small>Copyright Hampton Catlin</small>
      </div>
    </div>
  </body>
</html>
```

Pretty standard stuff. In this example (à la Rails), the yield part is where we print out the page-specific contents. Let's convert it the way that we know how so far.

Note: Try doing these next few steps along with us. Grab one of your sites, throw it into a tmp file and start hacking away at it. We promise it feels great!

First thing's first: rip out those pesky end tags!

```
haml/haml_h2.html
<!DOCTYPE html PUBLIC "-//W3C//DTD XHTML 1.0
Transitional//EN" "http://www.w3.org/TR/xhtml1/DTD/
xhtml1-transitional.dtd">
<html xmlns="http://www.w3.org/1999/xhtml"
xml:lang="en">
 <head>
   <meta http-equiv="Content-Type" content="text/html;
charset=UTF-8" />
   <title><%= @title || "Awesome Site" %>
 <body>
   <div id='wrapper'>
     <div id='header'>
       <h1>Awesome Site
     <div id='content'>
       <%= yield %>
     <div id='footer'>
       <small>Copyright Hampton Catlin
```

Much neater. Let's Hamlize it even more! We'll go ahead and get rid of the <div> tags too. No sense in wasting our time.

Note: For the HTML tag, we have to use the old-school hashrocket syntax for Ruby attributes. Why? Because the JSON-style attributes don't let you have dashes in them. Stupid Ruby hashes.

```
haml/haml_h3.html
<!DOCTYPE html PUBLIC "-//W3C//DTD XHTML 1.0
Transitional//EN" "http://www.w3.org/TR/xhtml1/DTD/
xhtml1-transitional.dtd">
%html{'xmlns' => "http://www.w3.org/1999/xhtml",
'xml:lang' => "en"}
 %head
   <meta http-equiv="Content-Type" content="text/html;
charset=UTF-8" />
   %title= @title || "Awesome Site"
 %body
   #wrapper
     #header
       %h1 Awesome Site
     #content= yield
     #footer
       %small Copyright Hampton Catlin
```

A few things to notice: when the contents aren't dynamic, you can just put them after the tag name. For instance: %small

Copyright Hampton Catlin. No equals sign means it's not going to evaluate it: it's just static text.

Also, we left the meta tag alone. It's ugly and will remain ugly. Converting it to a Haml tag achieves nothing. So normally we have to leave that, but for your reference, here is how to do a self-closing tag like that.

```
%meta{"http-equiv" => "Content-Type", "content" =>
  "text/html; charset=UTF-8"}/
```

We just put a / on the end, and the tag knows to self-close. So if we wanted to write <br/>, we can write %br/ instead.

We still have one really ugly thing left on this page—the DOCTYPE! Ugh. How many people just copy and paste from one project to another? We definitely do! So in Haml, we have a lovely little helper (named after one of our favorite bands) called !!! that does the job for us.

```
haml/haml_h4.html
!!!
%html{'xmlns' => "http://www.w3.org/1999/xhtml",
'xml:lang' => "en"}
  %head
    <meta http-equiv="Content-Type" content="text/html;
charset=UTF-8" />
    %title= @title || "Awesome Site"
  %body
    #wrapper
      #header
        %h1 Awesome Site
      #content= yield
      #footer
        %small Copyright Hampton Catlin
```

Voilà. No more ugly DOCTYPE line. If you want a specific output type, you can always reference the Haml documentation for a complete list of variations.[21]

One more thing: comments. Just as with regular programming, good commenting is almost always a good idea. If we want to do a nonprinting comment (i.e., something that we're only saying internally), then we can just do the following:

```
-# This comment won't print
```

---

21. http://haml-lang.com/docs/yardoc/file.HAML_REFERENCE.html

Basically, the - means it's a nonprinting Ruby line, and the # is the standard Ruby form for comments. So it's just a little hack to do nonprinting comments.

What if you want real HTML comments? OK!

```
/ This is an HTML comment
```

This compiles to:

```
<!-- This is an HTML comment -->
```

Index

The Pragmatic Bookshelf

The Pragmatic Bookshelf features books written by developers for developers. The titles continue the well-known Pragmatic Programmer style and continue to garner awards and rave reviews. As development gets more and more difficult, the Pragmatic Programmers will be there with more titles and products to help you stay on top of your game.

Visit Us Online

This Book's Home Page
http:/pragprog.com/titles/pg_sass
Source code from this book, errata, and other resources. Come give us feedback, too!

Register for Updates
http:/pragprog.com/updates
Be notified when updates and new books become available.

Join the Community
http:/pragprog.com/community
Read our weblogs, join our online discussions, participate in our mailing list, interact with our wiki, and benefit from the experience of other Pragmatic Programmers.

New and Noteworthy
http:/pragprog.com/news
Check out the latest pragmatic developments, new titles and other offerings.

Save on the eBook

Save on the eBook versions of this title. Owning the paper version of this book entitles you to purchase the electronic versions at a terrific discount.

PDFs are great for carrying around on your laptop—they are hyperlinked, have color, and are fully searchable. Most titles are also available for the iPhone and iPod touch, Amazon Kindle, and other popular e-book readers.

Buy now at *http:/pragprog.com/coupon*

Contact Us

Online Orders:	*http:/pragprog.com/catalog*
Customer Service:	*support@pragprog.com*
International Rights:	*translations@pragprog.com*
Academic Use:	*academic@pragprog.com*
Write for Us:	*http:/pragprog.com/write-for-us*
Or Call:	+1 800-699-7764